Barbara W
Wi

Ron Brown

ALL ROUND THE COMPASS

By the same author:

Beekeeping: A Seasonal Guide, 1985, B T Batsford Ltd, London (3rd printing, 1992)
Honey Bees: A Guide to Management, 1988, The Crowood Press, Marlborough (2nd edition, 1990)
Beeswax, 1981, Bee Books New & Old, Burrowbridge (2nd edition, 1989)
One Thousand Years of Devon Beekeeping, 1975, Devon Beekeepers' Assn, Newton Abbot

All Round the Compass

Stories from RAF Days

RON BROWN

Ron Brown (signature)

JANUS PUBLISHING COMPANY
London, England

First published in Great Britain 1993 by
Janus Publishing Company

Copyright © Ron Brown 1993

British Library Cataloguing-in-Publication Data
A catalogue record for this book is
available from the British Library

ISBN 1 85767 081 7

All rights reserved. No part of this publication
may be reproduced, stored in a retrieval system
or transmitted in any form or by any means
electronic, mechanical, photocopying, recording or otherwise
without the prior permission of the publisher.

Cover design David Murphy

Phototypeset by Intype, London
Printed & bound in England by
Antony Rowe Ltd, Chippenham, Wiltshire

Contents

Britain, 1937–1941
1   Pre-war life in the RAF   1
2   Royal connections   6
3   The friendly Anson   9
4   War comes   12
5   Kipper patrols   18
6   The Long arm of coincidence   21
7   Save us from our friends – I   23
8   Deceiving the Luftwaffe   25
9   Mining the Dutch canals   29

The Arctic, 1941–1943
10 Icelandic miscellany   33
11 Pack-ice patrols   38
12 Luckier than the *Bismarck*   44
13 Aircraft captures submarine   46
14 Flying the Atlantic by stages   54
15 Part of a day's work   58
16 Greenland and the War   61
17 B–17 missing over Greenland   69
18 Flying around Iceland – 1943   74
19 With a convoy to Russia   80

Mediterranean, 1943–1945
20	Fun at Gibraltar	89
21	Grim coincidences	91
22	Consol-navigation system	93
23	Foss Way – Gibraltar	95
24	No balloons for the admiral	99
25	'Met' flights and unusual cargoes	105
26	Save us from our friends – II	111
27	The Condors of KG 40	114
28	Flying airships with the US Navy	119
29	Battle of the Strait of Gibraltar	125
30	General Montgomery seen in Gibraltar	130
31	*Per Minimis ad astra*	133

Acknowledgements

To my family and friends of all ages whose interest, encouragement and helpful criticism have helped this book to emerge.
Also to my typist Anita Stokes for her skill in deciphering my notes and for her prompt and accurate typing.

To the memory of all those comrades
(including the best man at my 1939 wedding) who
failed to survive the war.

Britain, 1937–41

1

Pre-War Life in the RAF

My job before the war was Station Education Officer at RAF Bircham Newton, in west Norfolk, after a period of initial training at Coastal Command headquarters, RAF Lee-on-Solent. I had general responsibility for anything connected with education, from coaching officers taking examinations for permanent commissions to liaison with local schools in respect of the children of RAF personnel. I taught maths and navigation and with the help of NCO schoolmasters covered the range of the various promotion examinations, for example, from corporal to sergeant. Specialist navigation instruction was provided by courses at RAF Thorney Island and at the RAF School of Air Navigation. Most of our pilots were on short-service commissions and only a minority were Cranwell-trained. From about 1935 onwards there was a very rapid expansion in the RAF and the idea was to train a large number of aircrew in order to create a reserve later on. In the event, war came before most of these had served their first five years.

In 1937/38 it looked as if the future of civil flying lay with the big four-engined 'C'-class flying boats, so those hoping for a flying career were trying very hard to get transferred to 202 or 204 Squadrons (both flying-boat squadrons). As it happened, of course, flying boats became virtually obsolete before the end of the war.

I also had to look after the educational needs of a detached 'Queen Bee' flight at Weybourne, near Sheringham, which operated remote-controlled target aircraft – the 'Queen-Bee' – and drogue-towing for Army AA training. The Station Photographic Section came under my wing, as did the mess and station libraries; after a few weeks, I was also appointed Station Sports Officer. An early success in this field which gave me great satisfaction was spotting a reference in KR and ACI (King's Regulations and Air Council Instructions) to the paramount importance of swimming instruction to aircrew having to fly regularly over the sea. This enabled me to push through the provision of regular service transport between Bircham and the nearest swimming-pool (at Hunstanton, a seaside town about nine miles away), against the strong opposition of the Station Accounts Officer, who tended to guard RAF funds over-zealously, we thought. KR and ACI were contained in a large book (frequently amended) giving guidance on all kinds of RAF matters. It was the ultimate authority on most things. We were also ruled and informed by Daily Routine Orders (DROs) promulgated by the Station Adjutant daily.

I was naturally interested in flying and air navigation; in fact, I had unofficial flying lessons on the station Magister, a two-seater light aircraft. My tutor, Sqn Ldr Burgess, had been a flying instructor and wanted to keep his hand in. I also flew frequently in Ansons with my friends in 206 and 220 Squadrons, by day and by night, on various training exercises. We often flew on cross-country flights to other RAF stations, in particular Boscombe Down, where I remember being allowed to take over the controls of one of the first Stirling four-engined bombers on trial there.

For peacetime training, cross-country flights and photographic work, the Anson was ideal, as it was for navigation over the North Sea, armament training based on Leuchars, Fife, and night bombing practice on the range at Ackington, near Newcastle-on-Tyne. From time to time there were interesting exercises like finding and photographing the *Queen Mary* somewhere out of Cherbourg bound for New York, based on a general knowledge of her timetable. I still have at home a lovely black-and-white photograph of her taken at 0600 hrs one morning in June 1939, with not a soul visible on deck.

A well-kept pre-war secret was the development of Watson-Watt's Radio Direction Finding (RDF, or radar, as it was later called). The world's very first radar station was at Bawdsey Manor, five miles north of Felixstowe, in Suffolk. I remember one occasion early in 1939 when a flight of three Ansons had to patrol in close formation from Harwich to three miles offshore at The Hague, then north-east along the Dutch coast to Terschelling light and then back to Bircham on a direct course. Visibility was poor, about three miles, and it happened that one aircraft lagged behind by two or three miles. Within two minutes we received a peremptory signal from 16 Group HQ (Chatham) ordering us to rejoin close formation immediately. At the time we were at least thirty miles from any coast, with no shipping in sight. How could they have known of our lapse? Our understanding was that we were on some form of calibration exercise for a radio direction-finder plus observer corps in East Anglia, but of course it was really to give practice for the world's first radar station. Actually this signal (in plain language) was a potential breach of security; the Germans might have monitored our radio traffic and interpreted it correctly.

Having friends in Suffolk, I had heard rumours of Bawdsey

Manor and strange happenings to cars in that remote area. Like, for example, a car driving smoothly along a country road and having a sudden engine failure. This particular story featured a policeman on a cycle who, when asked for help, just looked at his watch and said, 'Try again in ten minutes, your engine will start again then.' The idea locally accepted was that the new wireless station at Bawdsey sent out rays which somehow short-circuited an engine ignition system. Obviously someone did a useful job of disinformation at this time. During the next two or three years, a chain of such radar stations was built at high speed around the south-eastern coastline of Britain, before that fateful summer of 1940. Without these radar stations, the Battle of Britain might well have been lost.

At a social level, life before the war at Bircham was idyllic. We shot and dined with Norfolk farmers and aristocracy. We sailed and played tennis with them and their daughters and they in turn enjoyed our guest nights and just dropping in for a drink in the ante-room. Our batmen really gave service; mine would notice when I had chalked my name on the squash-court board to play before dinner, and my gear would be laid out in my room. After the game my bath would be drawn and my evening kit laid out. Once-worn shirts just disappeared and came back washed and ironed. In the mess no money was ever seen; we signed chits for drinks and cigarettes. If playing bridge, the gains or losses had to be recorded in a bridge book and miraculously appeared as credits or debits on the monthly mess bill. When at official dinner nights, with squadron silver on the table, the port was passed at the end of the meal, an invisible but keen-eyed mess steward took careful note, but this was usually not more than once a week. In fact, quite often a night-flying programme would be laid on to coincide with a dining-in night, to secure its cancellation. Married officers living out sometimes regarded this official parade as a chore.

One interesting little incident about a year before the war was a forced landing by a Flying Officer Clark in Holland, due to engine failure, I think. He was so well treated by the Dutch that he organized a 'thank you' party by the RAF on behalf of himself and crew, signed the bill and told the hotel to send it via the British Embassy to the Air Ministry in London. You can probably imagine the correspondence and arguments that ensued when the Air Ministry sent the bill to Bircham Newton for payment by the Station Accounts Officer. In the end it was paid by the Air Ministry.

In 1938/9 there were still many links with the First World War, including a wonderful twenty-first birthday party for the RAF on 1 April 1939, held locally in the 'Duke's Head', King's Lynn, and no doubt in many grander places all over Britain.

No RAF Cranwell-trained officer had yet reached high rank, and certainly all Air Vice-Marshals and above were ex-Royal Flying Corps or Naval Air Service. Most Squadron Leaders and Wing Commanders – and Warrant-Officers – had served in the 1920s and I heard some fascinating stories of RAF life in the early days. I particularly remember when Group Captain Montgomery-Moore was staying for a couple of days with our CO at Bircham. I was privileged to be in a group around a log fire in the ante-room, hearing stories of the days when they were both in Mesopotamia (no Iraq in those days) and law and order were maintained by a couple of RAF armoured car squadrons plus a few de Havilland biplanes. This, I heard, was where our Station Commander, G/Capt. Harold Primrose, acquired the nickname 'Flower of the Desert'. Several senior NCOs wore the green/blue/green service ribbon of that period, commonly called 'King Feisal's

Medal'. In those days, the entire annual budget of the RAF was much less than the cost of one Tornado today. Stories of life at Shaibah and Habbaniya and songs like 'Those Shaibah Blues', illustrated a period gone for ever.

In the billiard-room of our mess at Bircham was a wonderful framed painting of a large Handley-Page bomber of 1918 (at Sedgeford or Bircham, I think), with a robed padre preaching at an open-air service from the open cockpit twelve feet off the ground and a large congregation of khaki-clad Royal Flying Corps officers and men.

In 1938 Sedgeford, a small ex-airfield about five miles away, still had old abandoned aircraft hangars from the First World War; they were used to store farm equipment. Local people still spoke of the end of the 1914–18 War, when contractors worked on for several weeks to complete hangars which would never be used, while other contractors were paid to demolish workshops a few yards away. One felt very close to the early days of flying and the birth of the RAF.

2
Royal Connections

As Bircham Newton was only five miles from Sandringham House, where the Royal Family spent so much time, we felt we were more 'royal' than most Royal Air Force stations. This brought a number of interesting contacts, in peace and in the early days of the war. In peace, we had to regard a three-mile air space around the house as a forbidden zone, and respected old Queen Mary's dislike of noisy aircraft. It was understood that she liked to sit by an open window and sew, enjoying the peaceful air of the Norfolk countryside. Her upright figure was well known in the antique shops of King's Lynn and Hunstanton, and her knowledge of furniture and her general shrewdness were much admired by the dealers. It was therefore with much delight that I was privileged to take part in a mock air raid on Sandringham in January 1939, as part of an RAF exercise.

Three Ansons of 206 Squadron were briefed to make a series of dive-bombing attacks at maximum speed, and the *Sunday Dispatch* duly reported in a front-page headline: THREE OF BRITAIN'S FASTEST BOMBERS ROARED OVERHEAD. We must have been flying at almost 200 mph in what we cynically called 'glide bombing'. Big deal! I think what we enjoyed most was the pleasure of seeing two little girls, about twelve and nine years old, standing by their white ponies and enthusiastically waving scarves at us, very much as my own young sisters had done a few weeks before in the small Cambridgeshire village of Brinkley. But that had been very unofficial!

As part of air-raid precautions, I also had to lecture to the Sandringham household staff on the types of German aircraft which might be involved and the probable effect of any bombs. I remember taking the station epidiascope and projecting photographs of Dornier 17 and Heinkel 111 aircraft. On one such occasion, I was entertained to dinner there by a Lincolnshire landowner, who seemed to be in charge of the estate. I think his name was Welby, and he had an elderly butler, known affectionately as 'Shuffle-bottom', who kept my glass well filled. At that time I was recently married and living out at Old Hunstanton, so very much appreciated being offered the freedom of the royal vegetable garden.

Before war broke out, another humble task which we carried out with great pleasure was to transport the royal dogs from Windsor to Sandringham (via RAF Halton). They were probably very well house-trained, but they were not air-trained! Small things like this could always be fitted in with routine cross-country flights, necessary for training aircrews newly arrived from flying training school. They were also good for morale. Perhaps in recognition of services like this, we were remembered when pheasant shoots were arranged in the autumn, and I recall with delight the memory of royal roast pheasant at mess dinners. At our official guest nights (pre-war) we enjoyed the company of Norfolk farmers and aristocracy, and the occasional unofficial visits of dear old Lord Fermoy, husband of one of Her Majesty's Ladies-in-Waiting. He often had difficulty in starting his car on a cold evening and we would turn out to give a hand.

In 1940, I became involved in the security of Appleton House, a few miles from Bircham. King Haakon and the Norwegian royal family had escaped from the German invasion and were to live quietly at Appleton House for the duration of the war, with complete absence of any publicity. One of my tasks in November/December 1940 was to take air photos and advise on the camouflage of new work being carried out there.

206 General Reconnaissance Squadron's duties in war were mainly coastal and maritime, and a further royal connection had to do with homing pigeons from the Sandringham lofts. We carried a wicker basket with a couple of royal pigeons on flights over the North Sea, and each bird had a small capsule on a leg to take a message should we have to ditch in the sea. They did not usually join us, however, on convoy escort duty, when we were in sight of the coast most of the time, but on anti-submarine patrol across the North Sea, reconnaissance

off the Danish and Norwegian coast and so on. I cannot remember offhand any occasion when we used them from need, but in training the idea worked very well. An observer at the Sandringham pigeon lofts would spot the return of a bird, detach the message capsule and telephone the message through to the Operations Room at Bircham Newton.

We were privileged to enjoy visits by our King and Queen, with their two young daughters, sometimes for tea in the mess informally, and on one occasion, at the end of 1940, for an official investiture, which was held in a large hangar and was followed by a sherry party.

Several well-known fighter pilots were decorated for their exploits in the Battle of Britain. The Royals circulated freely in the ante-room, the two princesses each with a lady-in-waiting. We were most impressed by their easy and fluent conversation. I remember a very young, blond fighter pilot, with blue eyes and a fine, long moustache, attracting more than average attention. How could Coastal Command hope to compete!

3

The Friendly Anson

In squadron use from 1935 to 1940, the well-behaved Avro Anson monoplane, made largely of wood and canvas, belonged in many ways more to the First World War. I believe it was the first aircraft in the RAF to have a retractable undercarriage, needing 148 turns of a handle to bring the wheels up. (Birds and bees had their landing-gear much more efficiently arranged a million years ago!)

Powered by two Armstrong-Siddeley Cheetah 375 hp engines, giving a cruising speed of 120 mph and 4½–5½-hours' endurance, the Anson was scarcely a match for the German Luftwaffe at that time. With a bomb load of two 100-lb. anti-submarine bombs, a fixed .303 Vickers 'K' gun forward and a Lewis gun (First World War pattern as used by 'Dad's Army'!) in a manually operated turret aft, it was not a formidable adversary. It was a very well-behaved aeroplane to fly and had no bad habits. In fact, I remember one Anson dipping its port wing in the North Sea and still getting back home minus eighteen inches of wing tip. One could not take liberties like that with a Blenheim. I never knew either of the engines to fail; perhaps one might drop a few revs on occasion (one of two magnetos not functioning), but that was all.

Working from Bircham Newton, our job was general reconnaissance, including convoy escort and anti-submarine patrols. Too under-gunned to fight and too slow to get away, our accepted tactic should we meet an Me 109 was to dive to sea-level and make tight turns as the enemy fighter approached. On one occasion in 1940 we survived several attacks by a pair of Spitfires who thought we were a Dornier 17 (*see* Chapter 7). A Hawker Fury, with half the speed and twice the manoeuvrability, would probably have shot us down.

Forgetting to wind down the wheels happened occasionally, despite warning devices such as two green balls on the instrument panel and a klaxon horn which sounded when throttling back as for landing. The latter was so annoying that most pilots pulled out the fuse and preferred to rely on memory.

THE FRIENDLY ANSON

As a last resort, the duty pilot would rush out of his tiny wooden hut on the grass airfield and fire a red Verey light to warn the aircraft that wheels were not down. In those happy days before the war, we had two squadrons of Ansons at Bircham, 206 and 220, and routine training cross-country flights fitted in well with other requirements, like fetching turkeys and hams for Christmas from Aldergrove, in Northern Ireland or wines and champagne from the Channel Isles. One of our young officers (Pilot Officer Le Marchand Huchesson) was born and educated in Jersey, where his father was Bailiff, and the local hospitality was fabulous.

One of my duties was that of Station Sports Officer, and transport of teams by air was readily arranged, one Anson for tennis and two for rugger, anywhere in the UK. To correct any false impressions, there were also rigorous training programmes of day and night bombing, dive-bombing (we called it 'glide bombing') and endless navigation exercises, calibration flights for direction-finding (D/F) stations, armament training, and so on. Among the more interesting (and valuable) was searching for and photographing ships at sea. Reserved for Saturday mornings were short and simple tasks like swinging the compass, air tests after major inspections, and so on.

In peacetime, we had fifty-one days' leave a year, plus one long weekend a month. Usually an Anson would be arranged for weekend transport to the nearest RAF stations – in my case Stradishall, in Suffolk, about six miles from my parents' home in Brinkley, near Newmarket – on Friday after 4.00 p.m. Another Anson would collect about 9.00 a.m. on Monday morning. Passengers had to wind up the wheels.

Unofficially we would sometimes fly an Anson 'hands off', just by redistributing the weight load. For example, to climb, one crew member would walk back towards the tail. To turn slowly to port, the crew of three would move left, to make the aircraft bank slightly, with one man back a few yards to keep the nose up. Although not officially condoned, this technique in airmanship was to prove useful in the war a year or two later in other aircraft, when controls were partly shot away by enemy action; the aircraft could be flown home in this way, not to land normally, but at least to bail out over the UK.

With a light load, an Anson was reluctant to 'sit down' and would float on for ages with wheels just off the ground before touching down. In dry weather a good deal of static electricity built up, and the first man to put foot to ground while holding on to the plane earthed it, with a muscle-contracting shock. There were no static discharge brushes or conducting rubber tyres in those days.

When taken out of squadron use, Ansons were used for communication work for several years. In 1944 I remember flying in one which wound up its own wheels when a button was pressed – a great improvement.

4

War Comes

I married on 12 August 1939 and had saved up most of my fifty-one days' leave in order to take a long honeymoon in France. In the event, a telegram ordering me to return to my unit chased us from Rouen to Paris and I was back on duty by 25 August. I never had the balance of that leave!

Preparations for a possible war had already changed my role, and I spent a good deal of time in July and early August helping to organize operations-room routine, with a number of ex-First World War officers already training for such duties. For a couple of years I had been collecting information and photographs of German aircraft, mostly from the weekly magazines *Flight* and *The Aeroplane*.

As part of my educational equipment I had (as Station Education Officer) been allowed to purchase a fine Ross epidiascope, which projected very clear pictures on a large screen, not from slides but from printed pictures, illustrations or photographs. Long before war broke out, I had been able to give illustrated talks on 'enemy aircraft recognition'. Before the end of August, we were on a war footing, with reservists called back, the operations room manned twenty-four hours a day and regular reconnaissance flights across large areas of the North Sea. Ships proceeding up and down the east coast were herded into convoys, keeping to swept channels inside the protective minefield (as yet only partly laid, but treated with respect just the same). Our responsibility was to give air cover between Flamborough Head and Orfordness, handing over to aircraft based on Thornaby at the northern end and on Detling in the south.

On Sunday 3 September 1939, six Ansons of 206 GR Squadron were flying a parallel track sweep over the North Sea, having taken off at about 10.00 a.m., not long before Prime Minister Neville Chamberlain spoke to the nation on the wireless and declared that a state of war with Germany now existed. Only five Ansons came back, and some days later we heard that our New Zealand rugby player, P/O Edwards, had been shot down by a Heinkel He 115 float-plane, which had put down on the sea and rescued him. He was taken to Bremen hospital with a broken jaw and other injuries. As the first British prisoner-of-war, Edwards was visited in hospital by Marshal Goering himself, who shook his hand and assured him that any member of the RAF would always be well treated. At that time, the so-called 'Old Commonwealth' was very well represented, and in our mess of sixty to seventy officers, almost one-third were from Australia, New Zealand, Canada, South Africa and Rhodesia (plus one or two from the USA). They were all on short-service commissions.

On that first Sunday afternoon, a barrage balloon broke away from its moorings and drifted across Norfolk, trailing a long length of thin steel wire which short-circuited some high-voltage electrical transmission lines. We telephoned 16 Group and requested permission to send an aircraft up to shoot it down. The answer was 'No! This might alarm the civilian population.'

Nothing much happened for several weeks, except for one or two false alarms about air raids. As autumn came on, we had occasional intrusions by single German reconnaissance aircraft (we were close to the east coast and fairly easy to find). The usual visitor was a twin-engined Dornier 17 ('flying pencil'), which occasionally dropped a stick of four 50-kg. bombs. On one such occasion, several of us were walking across from the mess after breakfast to ops and flight offices when we heard the noise of German engines and saw the usual four bombs falling in a line about 300 yards away across the airfield: '*crump, crump, crump, crump*', and noticed an officer ahead of us flat on his belly, scratching at the earth as if to get down deeper. 'What do you think you are – a bloody mole?' enquired someone.

During those first few months our airfield AA (anti-aircraft) defences consisted of four First World War Lewis guns (.303

calibre) sited around the airfield, with a few sandbags. On one occasion, a visiting red-tabbed brigadier (Army anti-aircraft AA) was with us in the mess ante-room, enjoying a sherry and surrounded by respectful young pilot officers, just before lunch. Once again, a Dornier 17 came over and dropped its stick of four small bombs on the airfield, about half a mile away. In a flash, the brigadier was flat on his face, sherry spilt all over the carpet, with over-solicitous young RAF officers saying, 'Are you alright, sir?' 'Have you hurt yourself?' 'Let me get you another glass of sherry, sir.' The Dornier, flying in and out of low cloud at about 1500 feet, was not fired on by the Army manning the Lewis guns, because no one told them to fire. Probably this was not so daft as it sounds; we would not have wanted them firing on our Ansons and Blenheims coming in to land.

However, things soon improved, and within a few weeks we had a couple of 40-mm. Bofors guns plus an Army liaison officer in the ops room connected by field telephone to the gunners, who could then be given some warning of an intruder approaching, and soon learned to distinguish friend from foe. In fact, they shot the bomb door off the next Dornier 17 to visit us, and one of them ran proudly round to the officers' mess with it. All this was still very lighthearted; several of us got an issue of rifles and rushed outside to have a shot, something like pigeon shooting.

During this same epoch of the 'Quiet War', P/O Greenhill, in an Anson, had a very brief encounter with an He 115 float-plane over the North Sea. Both these rather ungainly reconnaissance aircraft circled each other in First World War 'dog fight' style, until Greenhill got on the enemy's tail and opened fire, only to have the front gun jam immediately. But he was a good shot, and the Heinkel crashed into the sea; in fact, he photographed it (with his private Leica) in the water with floats uppermost and no signs of survivors. On his return, the front gun was stripped down, and only three rounds had been fired. Possibly this was the most economical kill of the war! Of course, there was a terrific row in the armament section, and for months afterwards every aircraft had to check guns and fire a short burst into the earthwork butts before take-off.

About this time, I was called out to the wreckage of a Heinkel 111 in the shallow water off Brancaster, and was able to measure the arc of fire of its front and rear machine-guns, with their 'spectacle' ammunition drums. I also unscrewed a neat little clock off the control column.

The mystery of the third ship in a convoy lane which was sunk by a mine passed over by the first two is referred to later (*See* Chapter 6). It was soon realized that this new type of mine did not explode when actually struck, but was actuated by the change in magnetic field when an iron ship passed overhead. As a refinement, it could be set to explode as the second, third or even fourth ship was passing, in order to sink the more important ships usually placed for safety near the centre of the convoy. These mines were mostly laid by Dornier 18 flying boats, and the shallow water off the east coast of England was well suited to their use. One answer to the magnetic mine was the magnetic Wellington minesweeper, commonly called the 'Hoopla Wimpey'! It actually had a huge horizontal hoop running around the aircraft, enclosing the wiring of a solenoid circuit carrying a heavy current generated by a Ford V8 engine plus DC dynamo inside the aircraft. This produced a very strong magnetic field, enough to explode a magnetic mine resting on the seabed many feet below the water. At Bircham in 1940 we had a flight of four Hoopla Wellingtons, commanded by W/Cdr Purvis. Flying these was a dangerous business, because the aircraft had to pass almost overhead, very close to the water, to explode the mine, which then threw up a column of water nearly 100 feet high, and there was scarcely enough time for the aircraft to be out of the way. An aircraft flying at 150 m.p.h. (220 ft./sec.) might just be clear, but the upward blast on the tail could point the aircraft nose down into the sea. The dilemma was to choose the height at which to fly in order that the magnetic field might detonate the mine effectively, yet to be high enough, or far enough away, to escape the blast. The depth of water was an important factor here. It was dangerous work, and W/Cdr Purvis richly deserved his DSO for leadership and flying under these conditions. Obviously no magnetic compass could function in such magnetic fields, making navigation difficult, but I do not remember seeing any gyro compasses until 1942; these were then only fitted to help in high latitudes (with very weak magnetic fields).

In 1939, bomb-craters were a novelty, and when RAF Cranwell was first bombed we had to fly an Anson over to photograph them for the record. From memory, they were just like those at Bircham, and likewise remarkably similar in size and shape to those that I remembered from the First World War, when in 1918 grandfather Howard drove mother and me five miles in a pony-and-trap to see the first bomb-craters in Suffolk, made by an off-course Zeppelin, also with 50-kg. bombs, I suspect. My father was serving with the army in France at the time, and was more familiar with shell-holes than bomb-craters, I expect.

In 1939, the 'Father of the RAF', Air Chief Marshal Lord Trenchard, was Inspector General of the RAF and came on an official visit to Bircham. For his benefit I organized an epidiascope show of photographs of First World War aircraft, projected on to a huge screen. We all enjoyed the authoritative comments on their qualities and capabilities made by 'Boom'

Trenchard, G.Capt Primrose and others who had flown them. Lord Trenchard had very strong views on the correct storage of aircraft 'dope' (cellulose acetate) used in repairs on canvas and wood aircraft, like the Anson, and of course, all the First World War aircraft. G/Capt. Primrose, our Station Commander, arranged that the dope store should have a can of dope left open, with some carelessly spilt, plus some general untidiness, which gained a well-deserved imperial rebuke (and made Lord Trenchard's day).

5

Kipper Patrols

In the first autumn of the war (September-December 1939) the fishing fleets (largely from Grimsby, Lowestoft and Yarmouth) which normally harvested vast quantities of herring in the North Sea were naturally reluctant to carry on for fear of enemy action. They also reported several sightings of German flying boats (Dornier Do 18s) and float-planes (Heinkel HE 115s), which were in fact laying mines and did not actually attack them. With a food shortage it was vital that this herring harvest be maintained as usual, and so arrangements were made for air escort by Anson aircraft of 206 Squadron, operating from Bircham Newton, to give confidence. Our local contact was Capt. Atkinson, Port Fishery Captain, Lowestoft, a man dedicated to the work of herring fishing in the North Sea. Most of the herring were caught in buoyed 'drift nets', controlled by small fishing vessels which had one sail aft to keep them heading into wind and a diesel engine to get them to and from the fishing area.

At first the operation consisted of flying around the area where the drifters were operating, with occasional low flights close to vessels, and a friendly wave. Then we developed a simple technique of dropping messages written on flat wooden boards, about two feet by four inches, with a 'tail' of cord with several cork floats, making it easier for the board to be hooked out from the sea. Radio silence had to be observed, so this was the only way of communication. The first message was to inform a certain drifter that the skipper's wife had given birth to a 7½ lb. son!

The second message was just a facetious comment, meant as a joke, but it was misunderstood and an over-conscientious skipper abandoned fishing and headed back to Lowestoft to hand in a supposed important message from an aircraft! They normally stayed out for several nights or until they had caught enough fish, but were never very far from their home port. After this we quite often dropped greetings from their families and a spirit of friendly liaison grew up. They appeared to gain much confidence from the sight of an Anson somewhere in the vicinity. As we gained in experience, we came to associate an oily, flat area of water with the presence of a large shoal of herring, and from time to time directed drifters to more profitable fishing areas. They soon learned that when an Anson flew towards them with 'wings waggling' or, more correctly, 'rocking laterally by aileron control', we had information; when we flew off in a certain direction for a few miles before returning and repeating the manoeuvre, they would follow and perhaps an hour or two later find a very rich shoal of herring. On one or two occasions we noticed the Belgian fishing fleet hauling in big catches just hull down out of sight of our own fishermen, and dropped a message board to say, 'Belgians catching herring twenty-five miles away due East of you,' and so on.

The main season off the east coast was from August to early December. In 1939 the drifter skippers had their most successful season for many years, and kindly put it down to help from the RAF. A skipper of the Lowestoft/Yarmouth fleet won the Prunier Cup for the record catch, and they invited me to come over and collect enough kippers for every man and woman (nearly 2,000) on RAF Bircham Newton to have two for breakfast, with their compliments. My 1934 Hillman Minx came back stacked up with boxes of prime kippers (and retained the smell for weeks!). Finally, they invited all aircrew who had flown on this patrol to a grand end-of-season party at a big Yarmouth hotel. I organized a coachload and we had a wonderful evening of camaraderie with the skippers and their crews. Towards the end of the evening, the hotel ran out of beer and whisky and only had port wine left. (We did not have to drive ourselves back!) It was a very good public relations exercise.

As an interesting footnote, HM King George VI, on one of his visits from Sandringham, spent an hour with me asking about every detail of these 'kipper patrols', including the occasional encounters with enemy aircraft over the North Sea; like that of P/O Greenhill, who shot down a Heinkel floatplane. I also described the Heinkel bomber (the He 111) which had recently crashed on a Norfolk beach and which I had investigated at low tide, mainly in order to measure the fields of fire of its front and rear machine-guns.

His Majesty, with more rings on his sleeve than I had ever seen before, was particularly interested in this and stressed to me the importance of this information being widely circulated among aircrews everywhere immediately. I faithfully obeyed this royal command. This was the quiet part of the war in 1939, sometimes now called the 'phoney war', when our aircraft on patrol over the North Sea saw the only RAF action. Bomber Command dropped leaflets and Fighter Command kept watch. I still remember with amusement the irritated Air Vice-Marshals and Group Captains walking up and down outside my office, wondering why HM was spending all this time with such a very junior officer!

6

The Long Arm of Coincidence

It was a fine afternoon in the early summer of 1940 and the escort of a southbound convoy off the Norfolk coast had been uneventful. In our Anson, 'B' for Betty, we had searched ahead and astern along the swept channel, exchanged signals with the naval escort, and looked forward to our relief, also from Bircham Newton. Suddenly there was an eruption of water alongside and around the third merchant ship in the line and she quickly settled: the following ships passed fairly close by, and the escort vessels spread out to seaward. The pilot remarked to his navigator that it must have been a U-boat, as a mine would have sunk the first ship. But the water is too shallow there and there was no real hunt, in fact the *Mirabella* sat on the bottom with several feet of masts and upper works showing well above the water. The crew were taken off with no difficulty. The ship was photographed by our F24 eight-inch camera and then our relief duly arrived. The incident was signalled to 16 Group, for C.-in-C. Nore, Royal Navy. Back in the Ops. Room at Bircham, the incident was chewed over for a long time, and it was only many weeks later that we heard about the magnetic mines which could be set to explode after any number of ships had passed overhead.

Next day, another Anson on duty off the same stretch of coast on a routine patrol, reported the *Mirabella* in position so-and-so course 170 degrees, speed eight knots, by herself, a fact sufficiently unusual to warrant a report. In the Ops. Room another watch was on duty and the report of a lone ship steaming down the Norfolk coast was passed on the teleprinter to Chatham without comment.

Half an hour later, the Duty Commander came on the tied line. 'What the devil are you RAF chaps thinking of? One day you say a ship has sunk and only the tips of her masts are showing and then twenty-four hours later, she's making eight knots in the same position!' Hurried consultations and much flapping of sheaves of signals confirmed all that the Commander had said. The *Mirabella* had been seen stopped and sinking the day before; in fact, the duty Intelligence Officer produced a photograph and her name was clearly visible on the bow. The luckless aircrew were recalled from the mess and cross-examined. 'Yes, we saw the masts of a ship sticking out of the water about a mile away, but it was the *Mirabella*, about 1,500 tons, that we reported doing eight knots.' '1,500 tons – but the *Mirabella* was much bigger, about 5,000 tons or more – let's see what Lloyds say.' The IO produced a huge book looking like an old-fashioned family bible – Lloyds Register of Shipping – and we had the answer. 'Get the Duty Commander on the line . . . Oh, Stephen, have you a Lloyds Register there? You have, good. Well, in all the world there are just two *Mirabellas*, one registered in Liverpool and one in Montevideo. The first was sunk yesterday and the other steamed past her at eight knots two hours ago.'

7

Save Us From Our Friends – 1

In Coastal Command we had many jobs and, during the early days of the war, one of them was to take aerial photographs of army positions and advise on camouflage. One quiet morning in December 1939 we were doing this from an Anson off the Norfolk coast, taking hand-held obliques with an F24 eight-inch camera and noting general impressions of coastal defence guns and camps. Not far west of Cromer we had spotted a row of newish houses which would not have attracted any attention if left alone, but the end pair had been painted olive-green and yellow in the official camouflage pattern, so we assumed that the houses had been taken over by the Army and duly photographed them. A closer look then disclosed a four-inch gun position, very well hidden indeed, right on the cliff edge. In fact, we would most likely have missed it but for the camouflaged houses. After taking more close-up photos we flew out to sea for a few miles to get a distant view.

'Prof, look at that section of Spits, they've just broken up to do a practice attack on us.' It was well done and they came in at two levels on a beam attack, with full deflection. 'Practice attack my arm, that was the canvas strip off the leading edge, the beggars are shooting.' Our fighters at this time carried eight Brownings in the wings and to keep a clean entry a strip of fabric was doped over the gun ports: this was blasted off when the first burst was fired. Bert, the pilot fired the two-colour Verey light, the recognition 'colours of the day', but the red-and-yellow flares didn't mean a thing to those fighter boys, so Bert dove the Anson steeply down and put her into a tight turn about 100 feet above the water. This was standard defence by an older aircraft when attacked by modern fighters. Again, the two fighters banked and came in on a beam attack. This time a jarring clang told us that we had been hit, but a Spit going flat out cannot turn in a hurry and they looked quite small in the distance before they could turn and come in again. Thank the good Lord we were not up against Gladiators or Furies, those tight-turning biplane fighters only recently replaced by Spitfires and Hurricanes. Our old Anson, with its top speed of only 150 knots flat out, could turn on a sixpence by contrast. I was determined to get some evidence of this and hugged the F24 to my shoulder as they came in again, catching a Spit in the act of firing. In between each attack we sneaked a few miles off to the west; the homing instinct, I suppose, as one might just as well be shot down off Cromer as off Wells.

One more attack and our friends disappeared as suddenly as they had arrived. We had definitely had enough for the day and set course across Norfolk for Bircham.

Our Wireless Op. had contacted base and as we landed a

few curious onlookers waited ghoulishly by the duty pilots' hut; few shots had been fired in anger at this stage of the war, and we knew that this little incident would be worth a beer or two in the telling.

Our Flight Commander had the armourers go over the Anson thoroughly but at first they said we hadn't been hit. Then a more thorough inspection showed some strikes, mostly through the canvas but one or two through the airframe. Not much for three attacks by a section of Spitfires, was it? Our Station Commander, G/Capt. Harold Primrose, got on to Group and then Command, and told us that the fighter boys thought we were a Dornier 17. We heard afterwards that they got two rockets, one from C.-in-C. Coastal Command (Air Marshal 'Ginger' Bowhill) and another from C.-in-C. Fighter Command for having attacked a slow aircraft like an Anson and failing so dismally to shoot it down. It was said that the Spitfire squadron came from Canada and that they were banished to the more peaceful Scottish coast to practise their aircraft recognition (and their gunnery!).

8

Deceiving the Luftwaffe

In war, both sides usually have some system of trying to divert bombs to a place where they will do no harm; in our case it was to a 'dummy airfield' at Coxford Heath, a few miles from RAF Bircham Newton. There we had a small bomb-proof bunker with a corporal in charge of two airmen (ACH, G/D – aircraft hand, general duties), who would light up a small flarepath (paraffin goose-neck flares) when told to by telephone from Bircham Ops. Room.

From time to time our own homing aircraft at night would make an approach as if landing, even switching on aircraft landing lights for a few seconds, and then opening up the throttles after the simulated landing and flying out to sea again for perhaps ten minutes before landing back at base in the usual way. This technique was developed especially against so-called 'intruder patrols' by single enemy aircraft, which occasionally lurked in the vicinity in order to drop a stick of bombs on one of our aircraft after landing. Often our local radar station would phone in to say that one of our homing aircraft was being 'followed', and then we would make a brief coded radio signal for this routine to be employed.

We even had piles of brushwood and rubbish, sprayed with old engine oil, which could be ignited to simulate the destruction of one of our aircraft. The three-man team at Coxford took great pride in their work, and were genuinely delighted when bombed, keeping careful records. I remember that during 1940 they collected sixty bombs at the 'dummy', as against only twenty-eight on our real airfield at Bircham. The technique was refined to the point of transferring 'bomb craters' painted on old canvas or tarpaulin sheets from Coxford Heath to Bircham, camouflaging the former, so that an enemy 'recce' (reconnaissance) plane in the next few days could see (and possibly photograph) the 'hits' on Bircham Newton.

In overall charge of this little sideline was our Station Navigation Officer, Sqn/Ldr Longmore (son of Air Marshall Sir Arthur Longmore, then AOC North Africa). I remember going with him to take the corporal and his merry men a bottle of Scotch to celebrate an unusually successful night of bomb-collecting.

We also had a satellite airfield for emergency use at Langham, three miles from the coast at Blakeney and fourteen miles ENE of Bircham. One reason for this was to have an alternative landing-ground for our aircraft, should they arrive back home to find an air raid in progress. I have happy memories of an occasional flight there with Dick Longmore, in his private Gipsy Moth, G-AFJT, to check up on facilities (and also to shoot the occasional rabbit, hare, pheasant or partridge for the table).

Before the war most, if not all, RAF stations had magnificent neon aerial beacons flashing their signatures in Morse code ('B-N' in our case). Coming home at night was much simpler then. When war broke out, this was discontinued at first, but then we developed three alternative sites a few miles away (like Coxford Heath, for example), remote from any service or civil installation, to which the beacon was moved and switched on as required for friendly aircraft. In peacetime, various Bomber Command squadrons had used our beautiful beacon and in 1939/40 were continually ringing up for details of its new site.

I felt that, for security reasons, this was unwise, so invented the 'Dorothy code'. Bomber stations were notified through official channels of the three alternative sites, each linked with an apparently innocent remark. The caller was required to ring our Ops. Room, identify himself so that we could ring back to check if necessary, and ask, 'How is Dorothy tonight?' in the course of a brief social conversation. The three answers were: 'At the Duke's Head', 'Out with Charles' or 'In cracking form' (with optional embellishments!), to indicate the current position. If not functioning for any reason, the answer was, 'She's not very well today,' (with possible reasons!). The real

Dorothy was one of three very popular WAAF cipher officers (with Betty and Helen). The Duke's Head was a hostelry in King's Lynn much used by the RAF and Charles O'Brien was one of my staff who had been a regular Army officer pre–1914 and had flown as a pilot in 1918 before the RAF had been formed. Obviously, our beacon was never literally at the first-named site!

Before 1939, RAF Bircham Newton had established a well-earned reputation for the efficiency of its medium frequency direction-finding (MF/DF) wireless station, able to give the magnetic course to steer for base to any lost aircraft within a few seconds. Within a minute, the operator would give an accurate 'fix' if required; this needed a quick phone call by them (on a 'tied line') to one, perhaps two, similar MF/DF stations, and simple triangulation.

The simplicity of this used to fascinate me. They had a large wall-map mounted on wood with three small holes at the MF/DF sites. Gummed around each hole was a compass rose, and through each hole was a piece of string with a small weight on the other end and a small pin on the map side. It just needed the strings to be pulled out and pinned at the correct angles to observe the point where they crossed (a small 'cocked hat', in navigational jargon), after which they were released and snapped back to zero, ready for the next customer. Our MF/DF was operated by civilian personnel who lived nearby, stayed for years, with no transfers or postings hither and thither, and loved their job.

We had no hard-surfaced runway, but a large and firm grass airfield, and in 1939 and 1940 many bomber pilots remembered our MF/DF from their pre-war days. We often collected several stray bombers unable to get back to their own bases, who stayed with us for 'bed-and-breakfast'.

9

Mining the Dutch Canals

In war, it is always the unexpected which happens, and in the late summer of 1940 more unexpected situations than usual arose. No one had ever contemplated the possible need for full information on the Dutch canals, their depth of water, trees or other flying obstructions along their banks; all such information could have been obtained very easily a few months before, but now Holland was occupied by Hitler and his invasion troops were embarking in large Rhine barges at several points, ready to invade England. Our task was to attack the enemy and inflict as much damage as possible. We used stick-fused bombs (to give maximum lateral blast effect) as well as normal ones. Then, out of the blue, came the project of minelaying by aircraft based at Bircham Newton, not only by RAF squadrons but also by dismounted Fleet Air Arm squadrons 826 (Albacores) and 815 (Swordfish) operating with us. It was necessary to brief aircrews on every detail of the Dutch rivers and canals, with any obstructions, to enable low flying at night to lay mines, which would not survive being dropped into water from above fifty to 100 feet.

Urgent requests for such information through the usual channels (16 Group HQ at Chatham) produced no result, although C.-in-C. Nore had ready access to naval hydrographic records. In desperation I said to G/Capt. Primrose,

'Give me a letter of authority and a handful of petrol coupons and I will come back with the answer in thirty-six hours.' An hour later I was on my way out of RAF Bircham Newton in my 1934 Hillman Minx (still smelling faintly of kippers).

I had previously telephoned Capt. Atkinson, Port Fisheries Captain, Lowestoft, and was with him a couple of hours later. He had some valuable information in general terms, but not enough detail. From Lowestoft I phoned the university library at Cambridge and said I would be calling early next day on most urgent RAF business concerned with the Dutch waterways; I stayed overnight with my parents at Brinkley, near Newmarket.

As is well known, the university library has a statutory right to a copy of every book published in Britain (as does the Bodleian at Oxford and, of course, the British Museum). I was well received by a senior librarian, who photocopied pages from a number of reference books. Rather surprisingly, one of the most useful sources was a book published for amateur yachtsmen planning holidays on the Dutch inland canals and waterways. In return I promised aerial photographs of Cambridge and in particular of their library. I had taken some in 1938/39 and subsequently had suitable enlargements sent, with an official letter of thanks. Later that day, the necessary information was being used to brief RAF and RN aircrews, and copies forwarded to 16 Group HQ, Chatham, for their information! For several nights we bombed concentrations of troop-carrying barges assembling on the Rhine and in canals and laid mines from low-flying aircraft.

Just how successful this operation was we never heard, but it was probably a useful contribution and, as everyone knows, Hitler first postponed and then abandoned his invasion plans. I enjoyed the use of some spare petrol coupons during the next few months and soon we had other things to work on.

When G/Capt. Primrose was promoted to Air Commodore, commanding RAF Iceland (C),* early in 1941, he took me with him as his Chief Intelligence Officer (also on promotion, albeit at a much more modest level).

---

*Iceland (C): A term applied on Winston Churchill's specific orders, to distinguish Iceland from Ireland (R).

The Arctic, 1941–1943

10

Icelandic Miscellany

Iceland is on the edge of the Arctic Circle and in winter the nights are very long and the daylight hours very short, so that flying was very restricted. In periods of bad weather there were many hours of boredom. We played all sorts of card games, from poker and bridge to rummy and Slippery Sam. Amateur concerts were organized to supplement visits by ENSA and we operated our own 'Forces Radio', for which we provided many items ourselves. A few lucky ones had Icelandic girlfriends, or *Stulkas*, but in the main we had to make our own fun.

What I remember best are some of the singsongs we had with the Norwegians of 330 Squadron, working with us on convoy escort and anti-submarine patrols. A typical evening would be centred around a huge bowl of rum punch. The RAF provided bottles of Rose's Lime Juice, some brown sugar and kettles of hot water. The Norwegians provided the rum, which was in one-gallon stone jars (a Norwegian naval issue). We brought our own food and pooled it, plus our own mugs to dip into the rum punch. The entertainment was community singing with occasional solos, and our contribution was mainly old Air Force ditties going back to the

First World War and the early twenties; for example, 'Those Shaibah Blues', 'The German Officers Crossed the Rhine', 'The Runway was Ninety Degrees Out of Wind, and Tried Bloody Hard to be More', 'A Troopship Just Leaving Bombay', 'Star of the Evening' and so on. We never really understood what the Norwegians sang, but from the raucous laughter which accompanied it, I imagine it was much the same: frankly vulgar, but getting frustrations and inhibitions out of the system and doing no harm to anyone (except local Reykjavik citizens, who complained if we went on too long).

Of course, in summer the reverse was true, and in June we could (and did) fly throughout the twenty-four hours, with no flarepath necessary. It was possible to read a newspaper by natural light even at 2.00 a.m. What we needed most (and often did not get) was enough sleep, with old blankets over the windows of Nissen huts at Kaldadarnes to make it seem like a normal night. In 1941 we had far too few aircraft for the convoy work we had to do, and with the consent of General H. O. Curtis, GOC Iceland, used 98 Squadron, equipped with single-engined Fairey Battles. This squadron had suffered many casualties in France in 1940 and still more when the SS *Lancastria*, evacuating their personnel and equipment was sunk in the English Channel. 98 Squadron was based at Kaldadarnes, which lay beside the Olfus river about fifty miles south-east of Reykjavik. Trained in Army co-op work, no praise could be too high for this squadron in their unaccustomed role of flying over the sea and working with ships. By taking over the close-range work, they released our long-range aircraft (like Sunderland flying boats of 204 Squadron) for work further out in the Atlantic. With no hangars or cover against the winter weather, ground crews worked with only windbreaks of earth, like pre-historic walls, about twelve feet high, to give some slight shelter against the biting winds. In summer there was excellent salmon fishing on the doorstep as a recreation, but overwork was then the main problem. It was necessary for someone to help organize the Kaldadarnes Ops. Room along Coastal Command lines, with the assistance of two first-class Army Intelligence Officers, to give twenty-four-hour coverage. This job fell to me, with Flight Lieutenant H. G. Vevers (my deputy) left at HQ in Reykjavik. Gwyn Vevers was an Oxford biologist with experience of Iceland but not of RAF procedure; he learned very quickly and did well. When we ran out of navigators and some task still remained, on more than one occasion I left the control room and flew as navigator myself. I still remember how hot the Fairey Battle cockpit was after four-and-a-half hours flying at 500 feet (the Rolls Royce Merlin engine was not made for this). One such flight was on 30 April 1941, an emergency call to look for survivors of a torpedoed ship.

Alas, though fit and still in my late twenties then, my body just could not go on taking this punishment and early in June 1941 I went down with exhaustion and pneumonia and was admitted to the military hospital just outside Reykjavik. Everyone was most kind and the AOC (Air Commodore Primrose) himself came in regularly with his W/Cdr Admin. ('Steve'). The three of us had worked together at Bircham Newton and had gone to Iceland as a team. By July I was back at work, happily at my real job in Reykjavik, extra staff having arrived from the UK for Kaldadarnes, plus 269 Squadron of Hudson aircraft (W/Cdr McMurtrie). I still have a patch of consolidation at the apex of one lung, and have noted with interest at subsequent medical examinations (Colonial Service, for example) that some doctors detected it and some did not.

In the spring we regularly had severe gales and I remember

one period when the wind in Reykjavik blew at a steady 85 m.p.h. all day, so that one had to cross the street on all fours. It gusted to 120 m.p.h. or more! In fact, on an exposed headland at Vik, where we had a radio station, the anemometer recorded 133 m.p.h. before it broke. The radio operators were confined to a small hut all day, and when one of them ventured outside he was picked up by the wind and blown over the hut, to land on their coal dump twenty yards away, bruised but otherwise uninjured.

At Reykjavik we had large Nissen huts used as RAF workshops, and the gale first loosened and then broke the wooden ends. As soon as the wind entered, the whole structure exploded under the pressure and the airfield was littered with twisted metal. Air photographs taken two days later showed damage resembling that of a bombed airfield, except that there were no craters. Although held down by screw pickets well into the ground and attached to both wings, our aircraft tried to fly. One actually flew like a kite for a few seconds before crashing. Fortunately we had acted on a good weather forecast and flown the Sunderlands and Catalinas to Scotland, otherwise they would have sunk at their moorings.

Even today, not many people realize that the main British Home Fleet was based on Hvalfjordur, a deep inlet on the west coast of Iceland, for most of the war after the end of 1940. When thought to be in Scapa Flow in the north of Scotland, our battleships were usually lying at anchor in west Iceland, away from hostile aircraft. The enemy knew this very well, and constantly operated spies whose main job was to report on the fleet and its movements. We picked up one Icelandic-speaking German with several hundred pounds'-worth of kronurs (the Icelandic currency), a radio transmitter in a suitcase and a very unusual codebook. This was a Penguin edition of *Maxim Gorki* (I suppose because of its technical vocabulary). For any word of a message he quoted the page, the line and how many words along the line it was. The word 'aircraft', for example, would be conveyed by a group of numbers like 45/17/6, meaningless unless applied to another copy of the same book.

There were also false alarms. One such took Major Roy Wise MP (Army Security IO) and myself plus three others many miles into the interior. We had picked up radio transmissions and cross-bearings had pin-pointed a desolate spot. On arrival there we found an apparently deserted hut and thought, 'This is it.' We burst in, Sten guns at the ready, but it really was deserted, with no sign of recent occupancy. Later, an expert evaluation of the false information attributed it to coastal refraction plus the effect on radio bearings of magnetic storms associated with the Aurora Borealis (Northern Lights).

On a much lighter note was the so-called 'Morality Committee'. The Icelandic Government was worried about friendships between Icelandic girls and soldiers, sailors and airmen stationed in their country. So it was that the three services had to nominate representatives to meet with three Icelandic members once a week in the Althing (Icelandic Parliament). These were the ex-Prime Minister of Iceland, the editor of their main daily newspaper and a lady author. On our side were Cdr Cummings RN, myself (RAF) and a colonel, whose name I forget, for the Army. We used to meet on a Thursday afternoon to discuss the oldest problem in the world and how to solve it. My contribution at one meeting was the idea that there should be organized occasions when servicemen could meet Icelanders of all ages, socially and legitimately, but nothing ever came of it. Fatigued by long meetings, I would go to our RAF mess before dinner for some refreshment, to be met by cynical brother officers asking for the latest news on the morality front! At least I did not have to buy my own drink!

Speaking of which reminds me of the fact that in the early days we had almost unlimited access to whisky from the NAAFI at six shillings a bottle, but no draught beer. It was obviously undesirable that young aircrew should develop a taste for hard liquor, and our representations on this were soon acted on. Draught English beer in kegs soon became available at a price less than in England, and all was well.

11
Pack-Ice Patrols

For a considerable part of the war, it was important to know the extent of navigable water in Denmark Strait, between Iceland and Greenland, a possible route for German warships planning to enter the north Atlantic and gain the freedom to attack Allied shipping. It was, in fact, the route followed in 1941 when the *Bismarck* and the heavy cruiser *Prinz Eugen* left a Norwegian fjord and were later seen and shadowed by two British cruisers, *Norfolk* and *Suffolk*, before the epic sinking of HMS *Hood* and finally that of *Bismarck* herself.

From Iceland, we operated ice reconnaissance patrols at least once a week to plot the southern limits of the pack ice. The Admiralty watched this very closely, and if ever more than about a week went by without an up-date, then a signal asking for confirmation of pack-ice limits would be received.

PACK-ICE PATROLS

The disposition of the Polar ice is largely governed by two main ocean currents. The first is the cold Polar current flowing southwards from the Arctic, from Jan Mayen Island and the Greenland Sea into the Denmark Strait, down the eastern coast of Greenland to Cape Farewell, then splitting into two, one half to the south and the other carrying on along round the coast of Greenland to the north-west; this branch of the cold current carried with it floating pine trees from north Russia, the only source of timber to the Eskimos living on the west Greenland coast. The half that goes to the south carries most of the large icebergs, originating far to the north in Arctic Greenland and floating down into warmer waters. One of these icebergs sank the *Titanic* in 1912. This cold water is also responsible (when it meets the edge of the Gulf Stream) for the extensive sea-fogs off Labrador, Newfoundland and even further south. In another sense, it is also responsible for the rich fishing grounds in those waters, as the contact area of cold and warm masses produces vertical current and an upwelling of rich nutrients.

The second main current is the Irminger, that north-western branch of the Gulf Stream, which carries warm water from the Gulf of Mexico up to Iceland and around its west coast; by this time, it no longer feels warm, I assure you, but it is less likely to freeze and usually preserves some open water on the west Icelandic coastline, i.e. the eastern side of Denmark Strait. As a result of these two currents, the ice in normal years is confined to the waters of the Polar current, while the shore of Iceland, washed by the Irminger current, is normally ice free. There have, however, been exceptional years, when the edge of the Polar ice extended so far that the Denmark Strait, some two hundred miles wide, was completely iced over and closed.

The normal winter and summer limits of the ice were approximately as follows:

Summer: From the coast of Greenland just above Scoresby Sound to the north of Spitzbergen, thence easterly to Novaya Zemlya. This means that the whole of Denmark Strait is clear, as well as Bear Island and the approaches to Spitzbergen, except on the north. This northernmost withdrawal of the ice is usually reached in early September, almost two-and-a-half months after Midsummer's Day: rather later in the year than one might expect.

Winter: From the southern tip of Greenland (Cape Farewell) in a widening band roughly parallel to the coast of Greenland, in a belt up to one hundred miles or more wide as far as Cape Dan (65°30'N, 37°00'W), thence easterly to within about fifty miles of north-west Iceland and via Jan Mayen Island to the north-west coast of Spitzbergen. Pack ice from the Barents Sea north of Russia also extended to Bear Island in winter.

At first, our weekly 'pack ice patrols' were operated by Hudsons of 269 Squadron (W/Cdr McMurtrie), but by 1942 we had considerable reinforcements and often used a long-range, four-engined Liberator of 224 Squadron, able to fly much further up the Greenland coast; in fact we occasionally flew well north of Germania Land (*c.* 77°N), to within almost 700 miles of the North Pole. As Chief Intelligence Officer, I flew as an observer as often as I could, and took many hundreds of photographs of pack ice, icebergs calving off in Dove Bay and the Greenland coast generally. The furthest north we reached at this time was 78°30', and a turn to port for the return flight made me (in the co-pilot's seat), on the 14 July 1942, the most northerly flying member of the RAF, well beaten a few years later by W/Cdr McKinley in his Lancaster 'Aries'. He also located the North Magnetic Pole more accurately, proving the Astronomer Royal's location to be some 500 miles adrift!

Apart from the ever-present wild beauty of the bleak northeast coast of Greenland, there were some other interesting duties from time to time. For example, on 4 August 1941, in the Hudson 'Spirit of Lockheed' of 269 Squadron (pilot F/Sgt Clifford), in addition to monitoring the pack ice, our task was to drop meteorological codebooks to the Danish weather station at Scoresby Sound, a settlement of perhaps 120 people. We included newspapers, cigarettes and chocolate as a gift from the RAF. It was a beautiful summer day; the waters of the Sound were dotted with small ice-floes, open to shipping (but there was none).

I remember that the contrast in air temperatures at the coastline, between a broad strip of bare land enjoying twenty-four hours' sun a day and warming up to over 60°F, on the one hand, and the ice-cold sea on the other, produced very great air turbulence and an extremely bumpy ten minutes as we flew low over brightly painted wooden houses and a small church to drop our parcels. The local population all turned out to wave.

Obviously weather information at this time was of very great importance to Britain (and to Germany), as much of our weather originates in this area. Our Met. Officer set great store on the regular flow of meteorological information (barometric pressures, temperature, etc.) from Scoresby Sound, and the codebooks were to deny this advantage to the enemy. The Germans did, in fact, try twice to set up their own weather station about one hundred miles north of Scoresby, via a trawler from Norway and supplies dropped by very long-range aircraft (a Heinkel 111 with extra fuel tanks and a Focke Wulf FW 200 of KG 40 from Trondheim) and these were the subject of a tiny 'mini-war'.

On another occasion (11 March 1942) I flew as observer and photographer in a Liberator of 224 Squadron from Reykjavik to Jan Mayen Island (about 500 miles NNE of Iceland). The reason for the flight was the unexplained cessation of weather reports from a small Norwegian detachment stationed there. We had reason to believe that the Germans had occupied this island, and of course in March the sea was frozen solid for miles around and no ship could get near. We could see no sign of life anywhere, everything was covered in snow, and the small group of huts looked unoccupied. I photographed Mt Beerenberg and dozens of views of everything. Alas, when we returned, it was found that the F24 camera had frozen up, and the film had gone brittle and failed to wind on, so all we had were three clear photos out of eighty I thought I had taken. As we also took weather observations for our Met. section, I noted with great interest an air temperature at 5,000 feet of minus 40°. I do not have to say °C or °F, because at this particular temperature they coincide! No heated or pressurized aircraft in those days, and I was working through an open side window to take hand-held obliques, so there was also what the television weathermen call 'a chill factor'.

The Air Ministry (Photographic) responded promptly with the introduction of a 'Muff, heated, electrical, F24 camera, for the use of', duly promulgated in AMOs a few months later. We may have helped by exposing this weakness, and perhaps PRU aircraft operating at 22,000 feet later in the war reaped the benefit of my camera failure at Jan Mayen.

My staff in Iceland included F/Lt. H. G. Vevers, a biologist who had visited Iceland and Greenland with the Oxford University Arctic Expedition a few years earlier, also F/O Nettleton, a mountaineering housemaster at Rugby. Gwynn Vevers was my senior assistant. He was scholarly, thorough and absolutely dependable. His great personal interest at that time was gannet colonies, and I remember photographing for him the top of a steep volcanic pipe in the sea off southern Iceland. The entire flat surface was white with brooding gannets, and we did a count from an enlarged photo on the basis of birds per square inch of photo and the answer worked out to something like 20,000, if I remember correctly. Nettleton was single-minded and his interest was snow, mountains and climbing. His expertise was put to very good use when a Wellington crash-landed on Snaefellsjokull, a relatively small icecap north-west of Reykjavik, and he led the rescue party. Years later he tracked me down (via the Air Ministry) in Africa and asked me to visit his school (Northampton Town & County Grammar) when I was next in the UK, saying that he had some Arctic photographs of mine, and would I please identify the places. A year later, on leave, I had lunch at his school, met his senior staff and pin-pointed the photographs. The best one, large and well framed, was on the wall of his house. It was of Hurry Inlet, a retreating glacier on a branch of Scoresby Sound, to the north, taken on the day we dropped the Met. Obs. codes not far away.

While in Africa, I contacted Gwynn Vevers at the London Zoo (where he was a curator) and sent him what I believed to be the largest stick insect ever (about fifteen inches long), found by a senior pupil at one of my schools, Kitwe Boys High. In return came thanks in the form of a book token for the finder.

Sadly, both Vevers and Nettleton are no longer with us; in fact, it was reading Vevers' obituary in the *Telegraph* that jogged me into writing down these war experiences 'while yet there may be time'.

12

Luckier than the *Bismarck*

HMS *Victorious* was calling home her Fleet Air Arm Swordfish, or 'Stringbags', as they were called, after a search for the *Bismarck* several hundred miles south-west of Iceland in the North Atlantic. The previous evening they had attacked her with some success but this time she had not been sighted at all. The sea seemed very empty to some of the Swordfish but in the end all but one found their carrier; the one that didn't, on the morning of 25 May 1941, is the subject of this story.

When no carrier could be found in its expected position the standard drill was a square search, and for nearly two hours the area was methodically combed, but there was nothing but grey, heavy seas and a sombre sky. The W/T had packed up and, with petrol only for an estimated twenty minutes more, the pilot felt at first that he might as well ditch while he still had power. However, hope dies hard, so he just stayed airborne and prayed. With only a smell of petrol in the tank he cruised on and on, just above stalling speed at about 1,500 feet, and waited for the inevitable splutter and coughing by which the engine would tell him at last that what the gauges had been saying for the last five minutes was really true. Then his observer called out on the intercom, 'David, look – what's that? No, more on the beam; there it is again. Looks like a small boat, but it can't be.' The 'Stringbag' slowly banked to starboard and flew towards the object. As the course was then SW into wind, a quick decision was made to ditch on the first run-in: after all that vast emptiness, even a damaged boat was better than nothing. The ditching was a good one, practically alongside. With added buoyancy from her empty tanks, the aircraft showed no inclination to sink. All three of the crew (David Berrill, Pat Jackson and Leading Airman Sparkes) scrambled out on to a wing and swam the few yards to the boat. What a surprise! It was a large ship's lifeboat in perfect condition but with no one aboard. A quick search showed her to have ample fresh water, blankets, food, cigarettes, rum and even some canvas which made an effective shelter and wind-break. What fantastic luck! A couple of tots of rum and the sudden release from immediate peril made them feel that they were almost home, but slowly the realization came that, after all, it might be just a slow death instead of a quick one. Action is the best cure for depression and a few calculations convinced them that they were probably about 700 miles from Iceland and perhaps 400–500 miles from Greenland. Iceland looked the better bet and with a few square feet of canvas rigged to give steerage way, a course was laid for the north-east.

Nine days later they were amazed to see another lifeboat on a converging course, and when they came together found a dozen hungry Danes from a torpedoed freighter. Food and water, blankets and several hundred cigarettes were passed over and then came a long navigational argument. The Danish crew insisted that the nearest land was to the north-west and the Fleet Air Arm insisted that it was to the north-east. Both sides stubbornly stuck to their convictions and parted company still disagreeing. The Danes made slow progress to the north-west and were never seen again. Four days later the Swordfish crew were picked up, exhausted and weak from exposure, by the SS *Lagarfoss*, bound for Reykjavik out of New York. They soon recovered and a few days in the hospital at Reykjavik had them fit again.

Incidentally, a check-up showed the providential lifeboat to have come from a ship torpedoed at night in convoy HX 126 bound for Liverpool from Halifax, and lost with all hands two weeks earlier.

13
Aircraft captures submarine

In nature, many of the creatures that live in the sea are the natural prey of birds that live in the sky, but never before had a submarine been captured by an aeroplane. In this case, the submarine was later actually used in battle against those who had built her, in the best tradition of naval warfare down the centuries; unhappily, the custom of awarding 'prize money' to the captors seems to have lapsed, and no such luck came the way of Sqn Ldr J. H. Thompson, senior flight commander of 269 Squadron, RAF, operating from Kaldadarnes.

Very early that morning, 27 August 1941, a Hudson of 269

AIRCRAFT CAPTURES SUBMARINE

Squadron, on its way to join a convoy on routine escort duty, had sighted a U-boat submerging, but lost contact in a rainsquall; the pilot reported this by W/T and was ordered to carry on to join the convoy, while the duty RAF Intelligence Officer at Kaldadarnes briefed Sqn/Ldr Thompson and his navigator, F/O Coleman, in Hudson S/269 with details of the sighting and the usual 'square search on e.t.a.' was agreed. In other words, fly to the spot and, if nothing is seen at the calculated arrival time, proceed on a series of expanding squares, each larger than the one before by a factor of twice the estimated visibility, making due allowance for 'drift' caused by wind. Coleman was a first-class navigator and duly arrived at the charted position – by an extraordinary chance, at the exact moment when U–570 decided to surface again about a mile ahead and in a perfect position for an attack. Thompson throttled back and lost height in a shallow dive as Coleman opened the bomb doors and dropped a 'stick' of four 250-lb. Torpex depth-charges, spaced at hundred-feet intervals and set to explode at twenty-five to seventy-five feet below sea level. It was a perfect attack, straddling the U-boat with two explosions on either side before it was fully submerged. By the time that Thompson had turned to come back over the spot, the U-boat (apparently undamaged) was breaking surface and men were seen scrambling out of the conning tower. He attacked with front guns (Browning .303) in order to keep them away from their guns. On the next approach the Germans were seen huddled defensively in the conning tower, making no attempt to man the main 88 mm. gun on deck or the twin 20 mm. on the tower itself. After another burst from the front guns and rear turret over their heads, a white shirt was held up and waved by two of the crew. As radio conditions were bad, Thompson gained height in order to get a signal through to Reykjavik; this was in fact received and relayed by another aircraft.

The immediate reaction at the main Ops. Room in Reykjavik was to divert a Catalina of 209 Squadron from another anti-submarine (A/S) patrol to the position, and arrange for other aircraft to follow up, while the Admiral ordered naval craft to the spot which, for the record, was 62°43′N 18°55′W, time of attack 1050 hours local time. In the meantime, Thompson continued to circle the U-boat, with an occasional burst of fire from rear turret guns over their heads to remind them of the situation. By now what appeared to be a white board (it was actually a chart) was laid out on deck as a sign of surrender.

At 1344 hours Catalina J/209 arrived to take over, receiving a signal by Aldis lamp from the Hudson. 'Look after our, repeat our, sub which has shown white flag.' For the next eight hours this Catalina mounted guard, but during this time several other aircraft engaged on anti-submarine flights or convoy duty called in to take photographs and exchange lamp signals with the Catalina. All that afternoon and evening the U-boat crew stayed on deck. I was personally on duty in the combined RAF/RN Ops. Room in Reykjavik, where another drama was being played out.

When a surface ship surrenders she stays on the surface, but a U-boat could perhaps make repairs and during the night quietly slip below the surface and escape, to sink more of our ships. Our aircraft had made it plain that, if the crew went below, the U-boat would be sunk, but at night the position would be difficult. HQ Coastal Command in the UK had very clear ideas on the subject and signalled, 'If surface craft unable to reach position before dark after giving due warning sink U-boat.' I was privileged to play a part in this and stressed to Air Commodore Primrose the immense intelligence value of a captured U-boat, quite apart from the boost to morale of the entire nation of such a spectacular success at this bad stage of the war; there was also the inhumanity of probably killing over forty German sailors whose surrender had implicitly been accepted. The decision was made to turn a blind eye to the official order and maintain control of the U-boat one way or another. Our Catalina was told to signal her by Aldis lamp that she must show a light all night, with crew remaining on deck, or she would be sunk.

In the meantime the two nearest surface vessels were the armed A/S trawlers on patrol lines to the south-east of Iceland, the *Northern Chief* and the *Kingstone Agate*. At 2140 hours the Catalina sighted *Northern Chief* and gave her a course to steer for the U-boat; just before 2200 hours the trawler made contact and took over. After dropping flame floats from time to time between 2140 and 2215 hours, Catalina J/209 lost contact. On that day sunset at the U-boat's position was 2042 hours and nautical twilight 2144 hours (local time) so, in fact, by the closest of margins no orders had been defied.

At 0135 hours on 28 August, HMS *Kingstone Agate* arrived and held the U-boat in her searchlight. Catalina T/209 arrived at 0340 hours, and at first light reported the U-boat crew huddled in the conning tower and on deck close by. All good drama includes a touch of agony and farce, and at 0655 hours a Northrop float-plane of 330 Norwegian Squadron provided both, by diving out of low cloud and dropping two bombs, fortunately near misses. Soon after dawn HMS *Burwell* (a four-funnel ex-US naval destroyer) and three other surface craft were at the scene. The armed trawler *Windermere* pumped oil on the water, but in gale conditions an attempt to board by Carley float failed. By midday the weather had abated somewhat and Lt. Campbell RNVR and two ratings reached the U-boat and were hauled aboard. During the afternoon first the wounded and later all the crew were taken off and ferried to Reykjavik for preliminary interrogation before transfer to Britain the following night (in a luxury liner, from memory, the *Bermuda Queen*, but I was only aboard briefly in the middle of the night).

By 1800 hours on 28 August the empty U-boat was under tow by one of the trawlers, not without considerable difficulty, and was beached next morning at Thorshavn, the nearest suitable spot. Doubts about her buoyancy had made beaching imperative. That morning a naval colleague (Lt. Cdr Crawford) and I hired two Icelandic ponies to ride across rough country and reach the beached U-boat. There we were met by Lt. Cdr Woods, captain of HMS *Burwell*, and informed that no one had yet gone below in the U-boat because of chlorine gas, which is why the crew had all stayed on deck. To me this implied a fracture in the pressure hull, with salt water entering the battery room and coming into contact with the positive plates of the massive lead/acid batteries. It seemed far more likely that her thinner-skinned buoyancy tank had been punctured, affecting her trim.

Throughout the war we all had to carry respirators in readiness for a gas attack which never came. So, with Lt. Cdr Woods I went down through the hatch and gently lifted up one side of my face mask to check the air. A very strong smell of acid vapour, but definitely no chlorine! Clearly some battery acid had been spilt when the U-boat had been rolled over by the exploding depth-charges, and we were ankle-deep in filth, compounded of vomit, spillage from freshwater tanks and seawater drained from the conning tower, a mixture livened up with a dash of battery acid. We were in the dark, but had strong torches. We did wonder if any booby-traps had been laid, or other self-destruct devices, but thought this unlikely in the panic. Anyway, I was in an Intelligence Officer's heaven and nothing would have stopped me now. In a large chest there were charts giving full details of minefields around Norway, Denmark and Germany, with safe channels into ports clearly marked. In the radio cabin there were still two lead-weighted books, but the main codes were missing. Radio sets had been smashed with hammers, but probably enough left for the circuitry to be reconstructed. The personal lockers and shelves above crew bunks were stacked with hundreds of letters from wives and girlfriends, photographs of families and groups. Many more were swilling around at foot level, with sandwiches, fruit, cheeses and items of clothing. One could well imagine the panic when successive explosions shook the boat, rolled it right over and left them in darkness. The tiny but comfortable captain's cabin was more orderly. I noticed an excellent framed watercolour of a German country scene; it was signed 'A. Hitler'. Could it really have been by him, or just a present? I had thought he was a house painter, not an artist. At that moment Woods saw the name and put his fist into it, completing the destruction with some solid object. A wasted opportunity! I found three brand-new Zeiss 8/50 binoculars in new black leather cases, also a fairly well-worn one, not in a case: obviously the captain's. I now confess to ripping out my respirator mask from its haversack, replacing it with the used binoculars in a new case, wedging in several pairs of black socks (property of Capitän-leutnant Rahmlow, but my need was greater than his at the time), and his photo-exposure meter. I left the U-boat empty-handed, as I had entered it, with my respirator case hanging from my shoulder. The exposure meter was later lost at sea on a Russian convoy, the socks saw me through the rest of the war and the Zeiss 8/50 glasses I still have at home in Torquay.

I also took away photographs of a merry party held aboard U–570 before she had sailed from Trondheim on her maiden trip a few days earlier, and identified some Norwegian uniforms among the guests. I passed these to the Norwegian Intelligence Officer (330 Squadron) in Reykjavik, who swore to hunt them down after the war, but I never heard any more of this. There were piles of Danish hams, German and French wines, French perfumes, cigars, etc., but I doubt if much of this was left by the time U–570 finally reached the UK. Back at Reykjavik I remember seeing an urgent Admiralty signal asking for immediate details of thickness of the steel pressure hull; I forget what the answer was but it must have been steel of remarkable quality to have survived a perfect attack by four 250-lb. Torpex depth-charges.

Very justly, one of the three pairs of Zeiss binoculars was presented officially to Sqn/Ldr Thompson by the Admiral at a parade held at Kaldadarnes. Another went to the Admiral himself and I understood that one had to go to the Admiralty for evaluation, but whether it actually reached London I never heard.

F/Lt. Charles Bardswell, my colleague at Kaldadarnes, joined me later in the day and carried on after I left, for many hours of thorough and painstaking work, in company with an Admiralty officer flown out specially. We owe a great deal to their persistent and conscientious efforts to sort out and index charts, flotilla orders, technical manuals, blueprints, signals and so one. Among the rubbish sloshing about, the Admiralty Intelligence Officer found the empty box of an Enigma cypher machine which had been thrown overboard. The padded interior revealed a slot for a previously unknown fourth rotor, a valuable clue for the cryptographers at that time. There were also kitbags full of letters and personalia for further study in the UK. They also retrieved the new Swastika German Naval Ensign of U–570, which was later presented officially to 269 Squadron and will long be an honoured possession. All these were transferred by boat to HMS *Burwell*.

One technical device I remember noting with interest was a de-humidifier, which not only dried the air but also provided several litres of fresh water per day. At that time none of our subs had such a device. Later in the war I noted that this had speedily been copied and was being used in our own subs.

After fifty years, I cannot remember getting back to duty at Reykjavik, but my log-book shows that I was flown from Kaldadarnes to Reykjavik in the station Moth T7106 by P/O Harpur later that same day. I probably rode from the beach to Kaldadarnes by Icelandic pony.

By 1800 hours the next day U–570 was under tow round the coast to the fleet anchorage at Hvalfjordur, to be moored alongside HMS *Hekla*, the engineering depot ship. A careful check by a team of submarine technicians revealed negligible damage; in fact, she should never have surrendered. One ballast tank leaked and the main electrical switch had been thrown off by the explosions, but in a matter of days she was in all respects ready for sea and proceeded to the UK under her own power, in the charge of Lt. Cdr Colvin. After some repair work and re-stocking at Barrow-in-Furness, she was commissioned as HMS *Graph*, with Lt. Cdr Marriott as her captain, and on her first patrol attacked and sank a sister U-boat in the Bay of Biscay.

I next saw Marriott at Gibraltar three years later (*See* story 29).

With the passage of time more and more old friends have joined the 'great majority'. 'Tommy' Thompson died, aged eighty-two a little while ago in his native Yorkshire; a well-written obituary in the national press gave him full credit for his capture of U–570.

14

Flying the Atlantic by stages

In 1942 Britain was the only remaining foothold in Europe in the fight against Hitler, and the forces of the USA were building up for our eventual landing on the Continent. In the meantime the air forces of the USA were joining the RAF in attacking enemy targets. Their own bombers (B-17 Flying Fortresses and B-24 Liberators) were well able to fly the 2,500 miles across the Atlantic, but single-seat fighters had a short range and were being shipped across as deck cargo on merchant ships, travelling in convoys from Halifax to Liverpool, and unfortunately at that time U-boats were sinking many of them. One ship sunk often meant the loss of eight to ten fighters, quite apart from the rest of the cargo. It was also appreciated that, should we be threatened again by invasion, we might well need rapid reinforcement of fighter aircraft from America, and memories of how hard-pressed we were in 1940 were still very vivid.

Plans were made for a five-stage northern route from Gander (Newfoundland) to Goose Bay (Labrador) to Bluie West 1 (South Greenland) to Reykjavik or Keflavik (West Iceland) to Hofn (East Iceland) to Stornoway (Scotland). No single leg of this route was longer than 752 miles, which was well within the range of a fighter, even without optional long-range fuel tanks.

Airfields at Gander, Goose, BW1 and Stornoway were already developed and in use. In Iceland we had recently completed a full-length runway at Reykjavik and the Americans were working on an even bigger one at Keflavik, which we had previously used as a grassed, level emergency landing-ground. The missing link in the chain was an airfield in south-east Iceland. Here we had used a level sandspit at Hofn as an emergency landing-ground for some time; now, work was in hand to upgrade this.

By May 1942 plans were well advanced and it was thought necessary for someone with at least a year's experience of Iceland and flying conditions between Greenland, Iceland and the UK to make contact and share information with the US Air Force in Greenland, especially at the new airstrip at BW1, at the head of Tunugliarfik Fjord, in the south. At this time I was on very good terms with Colonel Morris, Senior US Army Air Officer in Iceland (and a really first-class bridge player!). I had also flown with flying boats of the US Navy, based at Havnafjordur, south of Reykjavik. So, having prepared folios of airfield details, navigational aids, photographs, radio frequencies, emergency landing-grounds and various background information of interest, I flew from Reykjavik to BW1 in a US Army C-47 (Dakota) on 23 May 1942.

In the supposed absence of any possible natural airfield site along the desolate and snow-covered Greenland coast, the Americans had used their giant earth-moving machinery to remove a large hill (glacial moraine) out of the way and to construct a long runway with all facilities. More about this later, but my first task was obviously to call on the American commander or his adjutant, before starting any discussions. I was expected, and Brigadier-General Giles called me into his office and asked me how the American forces were getting on in Iceland. He knew General Bonesteel (Commanding General, American Forces in Iceland) quite well, as well as Col. Morris, and after a time said, 'Brown, I believe you play bridge. I'm short of a partner tonight – will you make up a four?' I replied that I was very fond of the game and more than happy to join in. Later that evening, after dining at the general's table, we played bridge well into the night, and seldom have I held such good cards. Our bidding seemed to fit and we bid and made a couple of slams in the first two rubbers.

Halfway through the evening, a minor crisis arose – there was no whisky. His aide suffered some criticism on this score. At this stage I explained that I always travelled with a couple of bottles, and sought permission to put a bottle of Scotch whisky on the table, regretting that I had no Bourbon.

'Brown, I prefer Scotch, thank you.' At the end of a most pleasant evening, I was definitely *persona grata*.

'Brown, would you like to see something of Greenland while you are here? Well, Colonel Walters here, my Chief Engineer, is going back to the States in a week and we have a PBY5A taking him on a farewell trip around.' Despite his bridge losses, Colonel Walters welcomed the idea, and I went happily to my bed.

I spent the next morning in conference with the Commanding General and his operations and communications officers, giving full details and photographs of airfields and landing-grounds in Iceland, and of operational frequencies, coastal lights, etc. I remember stressing the practical value of Radio Reykjavik, which belted out 'pop' music most of the day at very high power (100 kw) and was most valuable for providing a bearing via an aircraft's D/F aerial. During the war, all UK (and German) radio stations operated on phased simultaneous transmissions from widely separated sites, to avoid this possibility. Reykjavik, in a neutral country, just broadcast from its own aerials, and reception over the sea in a wide arc to the south-west was very good over long distances: easily the best navigational aid available, albeit an unofficial one. In the afternoon, I was taken on a conducted tour of the base and shown the graves of Eric the Red and original settlers from Iceland 500 years earlier, as well as the massive work involved in constructing this base.

My tour of Greenland is made the subject of another section (*see* Chapter 16), as it was not primarily concerned with bridging the air gap of the Atlantic, yet was unusual enough to deserve inclusion. I flew back to Reykjavik in a Dakota piloted by Capt. Gann on 15 June, and later in the year had the pleasure of seeing the first flight arrive at Reykjavik. It consisted of fourteen P-38 single-seat US Army fighters, led by one B-17 and followed by another: for all the world like a brood of ducklings, plus duck and drake. For me, this was an historic occasion, seeing the Atlantic flown in a series of five short hops.

15

Part of a day's work

Anti-submarine
At 0935 hours on 23 July 1942 while on A/S Patrol, Hudson F/269 sighted a U-boat fully surfaced in position 61°47′N, 16°13′W (approximately 185 miles SE of Westmann Island, off the south coast of Iceland). The U-boat was first sighted by its wake at a distance of eight miles, while the Hudson was flying at 5,500 feet (unusually high). Full use of cloud cover was made and the U-boat did not begin to dive until the aircraft commenced attack. F/269 attacked in a dive at an angle of sixty degrees to the U-boat's length and released four 250-lb. depth-charges, Mark VIII amatol-filled, from a height of about 100 feet. The stick was aimed about thirty yards ahead of the conning tower and the subsequent explosions were seen by the turret gunner to hide the U-boat from view.

No evidence of damage was seen other than a brown discoloration of the water, probably caused by the D/Cs themselves.

From photographs taken it has been deduced that the D/Cs (set to twenty-five feet depth) did not explode until ten seconds after the aircraft had passed over the U-boat, from which it is evident that they overshot considerably. It is considered likely that they 'skated' forward on the surface of the water before sinking, owing to the unusually high speed of attack (220 knots), which was largely due to the height from which the attack was started. The Hudson had not altered course by the time the D/Cs exploded, so that in any case the plumes of water thrown up would have been in line with the U-boat and have hidden it.

Considered most unlikely that any damage was inflicted on the U-boat.

Air combat

Northrop K of 330 Norwegian Squadron, while on fighter patrol off the east coast of Iceland, sighted a Focke Wulf FW 200 (Condor) in position 65°00'N, 12°00'W, (approximately 117 miles SE Cape Langanes) at 1303 hours on 23 July 1942. When first seen the enemy was about fifteen miles away and flying at a height of 600 feet. The Northrop altered course to intercept, climbed to 3,000 feet and carried out a diving beam attack. The enemy opened fire first with machine-guns and cannon, shells from the latter bursting short by 1,000 yards. The Northrop replied and closed the range to 300 yards, firing long bursts. The last burst was seen to enter port wing and fuselage of the enemy, and caused smoke to pour from his port inner engine. The Northrop broke away, as he was wrongly positioned with the enemy up sun, and the latter made for cloud cover towards the west. K/330 then climbed to 1,800 feet above scattered cloud and shadowed the FW 200, which was in and out of cloud at 1,000 feet. At a suitable break in the cloud the Northrop dived on the enemy from his port quarter and opened fire in a long burst at a range of 400 yards. The burst appeared to go high, and then his guns jammed. The chase was continued to the east until 1318 hours when the FW 200 was lost in cloud at 65°00'N, 11°00'W, his last course being to the NE. The enemy aircraft was painted a dark grey with swastika on tail fin; no special aerial or unusual features were noticed. No hits were received on the Northrop. It was observed that the enemy was firing time-fused shells.

Smoke from the Condor's port inner engine ceased after about ten minutes.

Considered that the enemy was damaged, but not severely.

Aircraft attacks iceberg

On 23 July 1942 a USN Catalina carried out a reconnaissance of an iceberg in position 66°40′N, 25°34′W (about ninety miles WNW of the north-west tip of Iceland). The iceberg was 125–150 feet high and 350 × 200 feet in area. The Catalina dropped two 345-lb. depth-charges from a height of 250 feet. These exploded about eighty feet from a corner of the berg and had no apparent effect.

Convoy escort work/pack-ice recce

During the week ending 25 July 1942 one large and ten small convoys passed through our operational area and were given anti-submarine escort as follows: 18 sorties by USN Catalinas, 13 by RAF Hudsons, 6 by RAF Whitleys and 7 by Norwegian Northrop float-planes, for a total of approximately 900 flying hours in the week.

On 23 July 1942 a Hudson carried out a routine check on the limits of pack-ice in Denmark Strait (between Iceland and Greenland) as required by the Admiralty.

There were many more successful days, but also some days when almost nothing happened at all. This particular day perhaps illustrates the inconclusive nature of much of the war.

Peacetime training – find and photograph the 'Queen Mary', 1939

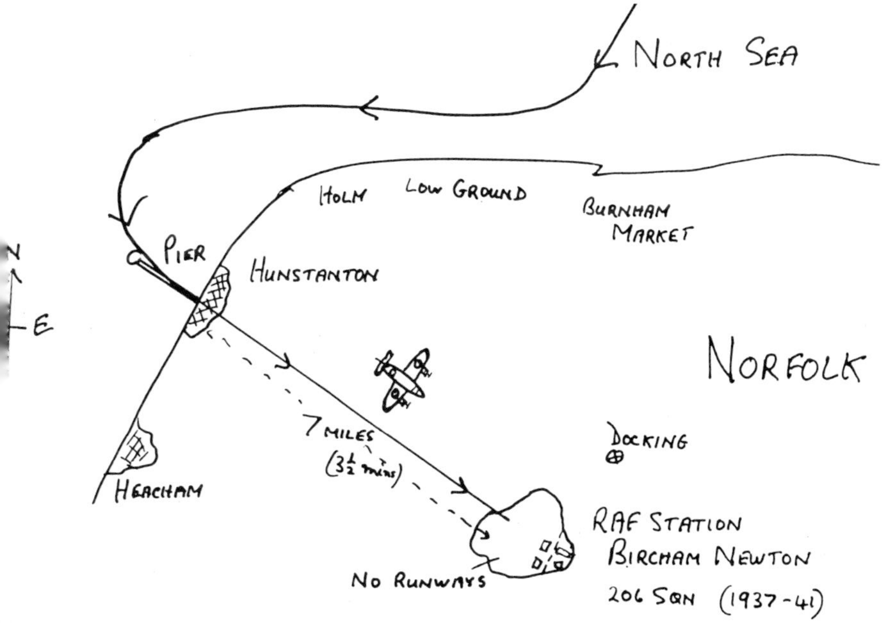

Flying home in thick fog

Group Captain Harold Primrose, C.O. RAF Bircham Newton 1940, A.O.C. RAF Iceland 1941/42

'Hoopla' Wellington

Iceland

Large iceberg, 100 miles N.W. of Iceland, 1942

Fishing in Iceland – Canadian F/O Pinhorn. While shadowing 'Bismarck' in Hudson/269 Sqn saw H.M.S. Hood blow up. Reported 3 salvoes long range fire from Bismarck. First over, second short, third two direct hits followed by huge explosion

Fleet Air Arm Swordfish

Surrendered German submarine U570 being boarded by Lt. Campbell R.N.V.R. in a carley float

The author with Col. Walter in Greenland waters

Col. Bernt Balchen's pets, Husky pups, Sondrestromfjord, W. Greenland

Flying the Atlantic by stages

Amphibious U.S. Catalina (PBY5A) rescuing B17, West Greenland

Glacier from Vatnajokull

De-icing a cruiser on Arctic Convoy, H.M.S. Cumberland 1943

Arctic pack ice

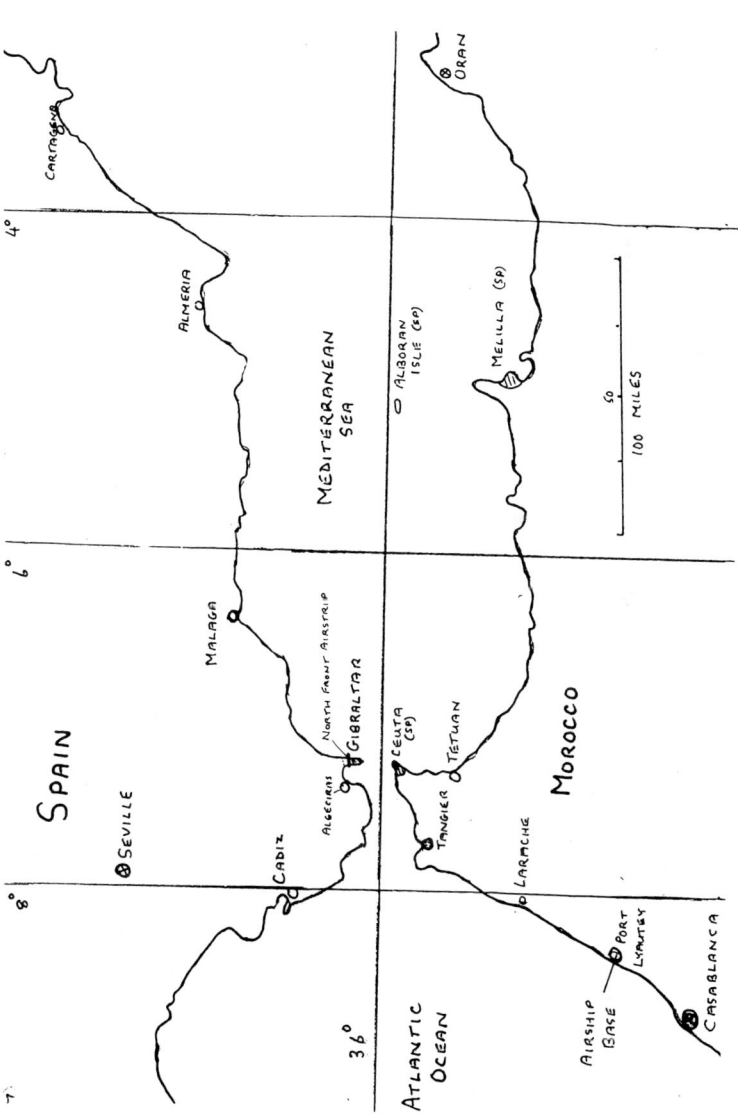

Gibraltar and Mediterranean approaches

Gibraltar, aerial view from South (*Courtesy Joint Services Photo Section, RAF Gibraltar*)

Runway being built out from old race course, Gibraltar 1943 (*Courtesy Joint Services Photo Section, RAF Gibraltar*)

U.S. Naval blimp visiting Gibraltar, July 1944. (*Courtesy U.S. Naval Institute, Annapolis*)

Squadron Leader 'Prof' R. H. Brown, Gibraltar, 1944

Condor FW200 – Bordeaux/Merignac

Beaufighter – long range

U.S. Navy airships, Port Lyautey, Morocco

Depth bomb dropped by U.S. Naval blimp (*Courtesy U.S. Naval Institute, Annapolis*)

Rear Admiral Sir Harold Burrough, Gibraltar 1944

16

Greenland and the war

Having travelled in both Iceland and Greenland, I feel that these names should have been reversed. In summer, most of Iceland is green, while ninety-eight per cent of Greenland is white. The only exceptions are a short strip of land around Scoresby Sound, on the north-east coast, and several short stretches of land on the west coast, mostly around Godhaab but also around Julianehaab, where Hr Christiansen and Hr Christoffesen were directing a small sheep-farming industry promoted by the Danish Government. I think they were fed as much on dried cod as grass, as on some Icelandic sheep farms. Since the occupation of Denmark by the enemy, the colony had become virtually self-governing. In normal times there were two governors of Greenland, both of equal status, one in the north and one in the south.

In the war, Governor Eske Brun administered the whole country from Godhaab, while Governor Svane (ex-governor of the south) stayed in the USA to cover Greenlandic interests there. At each settlement, widely separated from each other, there was a colony manager, almost invariably a Dane. Some of the smaller settlements had Greenlandic managers, but these appeared to have a considerable strain of Danish blood. A colony manager had duties and powers which were almost patriarchal. At Godhaab, there were two foreign consuls, Mr

Penfield (USA) and Mr Dunbar (Canada). Incidentally, the local population prefer to be called 'Greenlanders' rather than 'Eskimos', and I think consider themselves rather superior to their brethren in Arctic Canada.

Our first visit (Col. Walter and myself) was by sea in US Army Transport *Armstrong* to the island of Gamatrond, at the entrance to the fjord; here we inspected naval radio installations and defences under Commander Boucheron USN. He was a great character, of French extraction, wearing a goatee beard and known throughout Greenland as 'Boucheron from Gamatrond'. From here, we sailed next day to Julianehaab, called on colony manager Hr Andersen, and radio station manager Hr Thane and met all the Danish officials. I signed the official visitors' book, and noted that I was the first RAF officer to do so. One signature on the same page, only a few names up, was that of Marshal Balbo of the Italian Air Force, who had made a world trip with some flying boats a few years previously and had publicly declared, after flying round the Greenland coast, that there was no possible site there for an airfield.

We were royally entertained that evening at a dinner and dance hosted by Hr Andersen. I had an interesting conversation with sheep manager Hr Christiansen, as I was surprised that such a venture was even possible. He bemoaned the fact that he could not sell any lamb or sheep meat to the Americans, as they only ate beef. I told him it was just the same in Iceland. In conversation generally with the Danes, I asked what happened in the long winters, when they were completely isolated for months at a time. They answered that they looked forward to it, as this freed them from a constant succession of official visitors from Denmark. In the winter they dined at each other's houses, played bridge, had musical evenings, listened to radio and were very content. I was told that, in the Danish Civil Service, each year in Greenland counted as two years for pension and retirement purposes. Years later I quoted this precedent to our own Colonial Service apropos of service in remote Northern Rhodesia, but to no avail!

A very contrary view was expressed by Alise, the young and charming wife of Hr Brun, the Danish school inspector who was, unfortunately, away for a few days on official business. She pined for the restaurants and night life of Copenhagen, and was a very good dancer. When I surfaced for breakfast at the Andersen home next morning after nearly five hours' sleep, she called round with a signed copy of her husband's illustrated reading book for Eskimo children, in their own language; I have it still.

During the next four days, we travelled by sea, visiting Simiatak Island (BW3) and Narsak (halfway up Brede Fjord), inspecting naval and army installations and the US Coastguard vessel *Mohawk*, as well as managers and officials of a few small settlements. We returned to BW1 by sea on 1 June and with the Commanding General made a full inspection of the base and also attended the funeral of a US soldier accidentally shot. I had to give a talk on the work of the RAF in Iceland, but the questions they asked were all about the RAF in the summer of 1940 and about German bombing. I discussed security matters with Base Command S–2, and Air Sea Rescue (ASR) techniques with USN Coastguards. We had pioneered ASR at RAF Bircham Newton, from where my old friend Archie Tanburn went to Coastal Command HQ to take charge of ASR for the RAF in Britain.

Next day Colonel Walter and I embarked on US Army Transport *Dorchester* and sailed for Ivigtut (BW7), where a Danish population of 150 men was chiefly employed in the cryolite mine (manager Hr Corps). Cryolite is an important ore of aluminium not found in any quantity anywhere else in the world. Its importance lies in its use as a flux in the manufacture of aluminium from more common ores, like bauxite, enabling this to be melted and electrolysed at a much lower temperature and cost.

The mine at Ivigtut is geologically unique, as the mineral occurs in a deep and solid deposit, pure and easy to mine. I was given a nine-pound block of it, machined to a perfect shape and resembling ice, without a single particle of foreign matter. It sits on the table as I write. The entire output was taken by the Philadelphia Luminum Corporation and a firm in Canada, at a high price. Danish miners there enjoyed very high pay, with generous leave and pension rights. Many of them had their own motorboats and Greenlandic girlfriends living a mile or two down the fjord; they seemed very contented with their life. Here I also had a conference aboard the USS *Bear* with Capt. Crowford and Lt. Lee Roy, on security and strategic problems in north-east Greenland. This was repeated on our arrival at BW8, at the head of Sondre Stromfjord, and again when we flew by PBY5A to USS *Northland* anchored at the head of the fjord about one hundred miles away, when I met Capt. Von Paulsen, (Senior Officer Present Afloat (SOPA)), he was very interested in our ice reconnaissance patrols.

Next day we returned to BW8 (Col. Balchen), where, at the request of Col. Walter (i/c Corps of Engineers) I gave a forty-minute talk to 500 US engineering personnel on difficulties met in construction work in Iceland and how these were tackled at Kaldadarnes in the autumn of 1940 without any heavy machinery. I have a distant memory of a very lively evening spent with these gallant engineers, with a singsong to which I had to contribute. They had a college song, 'I'm a played-out wreck from Georgia Tech. and a helluvan engineer – A helluva, helluva, helluvan engineer' and much more besides.

On 9 June, while talking over coffee to Bernt Balchen about the work of Norwegian Squadron 330 (Northrop float-planes) in Iceland (he was Norwegian), there came the sudden news of a weak signal from a B–17 down in distress (*see* Chapter 17). Next day we flew back to BW8 and the following day flew (with Col. Walter) in our PBY5A to Godhaab. We stayed here two days with Hr Eske Brun and Jim Penfield and enjoyed many interesting discussions and local visits.

While in Godhaab, as a former Education Officer I was invited to the graduation ceremony at the only high school in Greenland. It had an intake only every other year, a novel idea for handling uneconomically small numbers. This year a Greenlander girl had graduated in the top four, the first time this had happened, and so was due to proceed routinely to Copenhagen for pre-university and university education. She was obviously delighted.

I pressed for information about the local Eskimo population, which at this time of year (having twenty-four-hour daylight) I would have expected to find dispersed more widely on seal-hunting expeditions. I was told that during the last fifteen to twenty years a branch of the Gulf Stream seemed to have brought warmer (or less cold!) water up the local coast, bringing with it vast numbers of cod. Fishing for cod was replacing the old habit of seal-hunting, and our new friends deprecated this, as age-old skills were being lost, and one day the less cold water might go away and take the cod with it. Nevertheless, I managed to find out that a party of hunters had actually seen the distressed B–17 land, but hid, then went away. They had said they feared it was German and might shoot them. Jim Penfield agreed that it would be worthwhile to spread around the message that Germany was too far away and that all aircraft would be friendly and needing help if they came down away from the camp. I also found out that the Danish civil authorities operated a comprehensive radio communication service network, linking all settlements for five minutes on the hour. They readily agreed to publicise the friendly nature of any aircraft and that rewards would be forthcoming in respect of any help given.

In general terms, it seemed to be the policy of both the US and the Danes to have a minimum of contact between their armed forces and the local population. In general this made a great deal of sense. However, with groups of short-range fighter aircraft expected to be flying to Europe via Greenland, there was always the possibility of a stray crash-landing somewhere, and local help could be essential in saving life.

Before I left for BW1, my namesake, Eske Brun, presented me with the largest and finest of the year's crop of ivory narwhal tusks (only sixteen in all). I have it at home still, and my daughter has the polar-bear skin presented to me at Julianehaab.

Back at BW1, I met newly arrived Col. Wimsatt, appointed CG-designate and expected to take over shortly, and at his request discussed the general situation in Greenland, especially the possibility of enemy action originating from any base they might set up in north-east Greenland, familiar ground from our Iceland-based pack-ice patrols. We also discussed ASR organization around Greenland. On 15 June, I flew back to Iceland.

Notes on discussions with Capt. Von Paulsen, USN SOPA Greenland

Capt. Von Paulsen stated that he was very interested in ice conditions off the east coast of Greenland, as he was in charge of the movements of shipping up the coast. No information had ever reached him from Iceland on this subject. I outlined the type of information which was available as a result of aircraft ice reconnaissance carried out from Iceland and Capt. Von Paulsen said that this would be of very great value to him. It was agreed that the correct channel would be from US Navy, Iceland to SOPA Greenland and, at the latter's request, agreed to make sure that USN Iceland received such reports from the RAF and to ask them to pass the reports to SOPA Greenland.

I then referred to the occasional movement of shipping up the east Greenland coast and said that RAF Iceland never received advice of such movements; the previous fall a large, three-masted schooner had been sighted off Scoresby Sound by an RAF Hudson; it might have sailed from occupied Norway for all that RAF Iceland knew to the contrary. SOPA promised to pass to USN Iceland (for the RAF) details of all future shipping movements.

The question of what vessels, if any, were based on east Greenland was then discussed, and Capt. Von Paulsen stated that, except for one small motor fishing-boat (similar to the very small Icelandic type), nothing larger than a 20-ft. motor-boat existed legitimately off east Greenland, and anything larger could be regarded as hostile and attacked, instead of merely being reported and probably missed on the subsequent strike sortie.

I then gave details of the types of German aircraft which might conceivably be met off north-east Greenland and also of the types of US and RAF planes which might be seen up there. SOPA promised to send photographs of *North Land*, *North Star*, *Bear* and other US Coastguard vessels under his command to RAF Iceland to assist in the briefing of aircrew for sorties west of Iceland.

Capt. Von Paulsen gave an account of his visit to northeast Greenland the previous autumn in the *North Land*, and said that the masts of the radio station found there in course of erection by the Germans had been broken and jettisoned at sea. Any wireless masts seen up there of any size, would indicate that another station had been set up by the enemy. The sledge patrol established last autumn to cover north-east Greenland during the winter and spring had not reported any activity, but in view of the immense size of the area, and the small number of sorties made, this was not to be relied upon too much. One of the trappers living up in the area had been assisting the enemy's small expedition last summer, but was considered harmless. Another trapper had avoided the patrol vessel and had not been contacted. Two US coastguards had been left at Halls Inlet, Jameson's Land; otherwise no service personnel existed north of Angmagssalik.

Summary of Intelligence left behind with Commanding Officers of BW1 and BW8
Air maps of Iceland.
Large-scale maps of SW Iceland and the Reykjavik area.
Diagrams and plans of airfields, emergency landing-grounds and seaplane alighting areas.
Photographic mosaics of aerodromes and emergency landing-grounds.
Dimensions of runways and facilities available at airfields.
Full details of positions and characteristics of all visual beacons around coast of Iceland.

Schedules and full details of the Icelandic radio beacons.
Schedule and data concerning the commercial radio station at Reykjavik, which now has a power of 100 kw. (as a navigational facility).
Chart showing positions and frequencies of all RAF signal stations in Iceland.

17

B–17 missing over Greenland

In mid-August 1941 the ice was beginning to break up in Sondre Stromfjord, well north of the Arctic Circle, on the west coast of Greenland. The first tanker of the year had not yet come through and a squadron of PBY5As was still grounded at BW8.

As their first RAF visitor I had flown in with a C–47 (Dakota) carrying stores and was staying over for a few days with Bernt Balchen, then aged forty-one and commanding the base as a US colonel. What a man he was: built like a barrel, Olympic ski-ing champion, amateur boxer, Admiral Byrd's pilot in the Antarctic a year or two before and still as Norwegian as they come. His idea of a forty-eight-hour leave was to take a team of dogs up on the icecap and disappear. Over a coffee on my third day there, we were talking about the problem of fighter reinforcements getting over to Britain and cursing the fact that hundreds were being shipped as deck cargo in slow convoys and getting sunk in the Atlantic instead of shooting down the Heinkels and Dorniers.

The wire-screen mosquito door rattled and a radio man burst in. 'Colonel, sir, there's a B–17 [Flying Fortress] in trouble out there; we've gotten a third-class bearing on her 195 True but can't raise her.' Bernt was on his feet giving orders in an instant. No planes had flown for days but by draining the tanks of all the aircraft on the base there was enough gasoline to fly a Catalina (VP 93/3) for nine hours. 'Squadron Leader Brown, will you come with me?' 'Yes, sirrr, I'll be right over.' We took off within an hour and headed down the fjord, dodged Simiatak Island and gained height while getting back on to that plotted bearing. The distress signal had been very weak, so we knew the aircraft was either down somewhere or else a long way to the south. Nothing had been expected at the base, so probably it was an aircraft in transit between Reykjavik and Gander, Newfoundland. What hope could there be for them? The best brains of aviation had explored this very coast for years without finding even a possible emergency landing-ground. The Italian Marshal Balbo, Lindberg, the British Arctic Air Route Expedition and now the US Air Force had all said that there was no possible landing-strip from Angmagssalik to Godhaab. An airfield in south Greenland would mean that even fighters could fly the Atlantic in short hops, from Labrador to Greenland to Iceland to Scotland. This was why the US engineers, with huge machines, had almost removed a mountain to make an artificial airstrip north of Julianehaab, at the head of Tunugliarfik Fjord. But the great icecap sat like a white jungle on iron-hard mountains right to the coast, here and there spilling over into the sea in crevassed glaciers. Had they crashed in some half-hidden valley, yet by some miracle survived and managed to get an emergency transmitter working? Or had they been flying and perhaps crashed into the sea even before we had taken off? We flew past Godhaab, with its brightly painted wooden houses and the Danish flag flying; snow was still lying here and there wherever the weak sun had not reached. At anchor were the Danish survey vessel and one or two sealers. I sat in the co-pilot's seat, with Bernt flying, and we followed the edge of the icecap, with visibility only moderate and getting worse as we flew further south. Here and there the bleak rocks pushed through, and occasionally quite large tongues of bare earth showed snow only on their northern faces. Bernt kept checking his gauges and finally turned to me. 'We must go back soon. Five minutes, that is all.' Our eyes were skinned but hope was dying.

Bernt saw her a moment before I did – 'There she is, look, sitting on that runway,' he said.

It did look like a runway, too, a good thousand yards long on a sort of plateau about seventy-five feet up from the adjacent sea. There was an area of calm water with only a few bits of ice in the lee of this finger of land and Bernt put the Cat down with cool skill; we taxied inshore and got an anchor out. The bottom was firm and sandy so we waded ashore and climbed up the steep side of the glacial moraine, for that was what it was.

The Flying Fortress had made a perfect wheel-down landing and the crew were standing by the plane, quite OK but weak. They had no food aboard except tinned Icelandic fish and a box of grapefruit which should have been left in Reykjavik. We sent our radio-man back to the Catalina to work Godhaab and ask for some 100-octane petrol to be sent out to our position, which for the record was 63°25′N 51°15′W, now called Ikerasarsuk. Godhaab was only some fifty miles away, so in a few hours a diesel fishing-boat turned up, plus petrol, with Jim Penfield, the American Consul. We all had a lovely fry-up of seal liver and blubber, with bread and coffee, and out came the story.

The Fort had had compass trouble and lost herself thoroughly somewhere to the south of Greenland; there was a magnetic storm and no radio bearing could be obtained, so they just flew along the bleak coastline, hoping for a break, not knowing that there was supposed to be no place where they could possibly land. To add to their troubles, the visibility dropped and patches of fog built up. An hour after their gas tanks should have been empty they tried to climb above the fog and lost visual contact. Then an engine spluttered and they thought, 'This is it, boys.' The pilot throttled back, put the nose down and the engine recovered, but all knew that they could not stay up for more than a minute or two. This was the moment of truth, and the moment for prayer. Then, losing height gently, they broke into the clear at eight hundred feet and right before them was this 'runway' – and, what's more, they were just about on the correct approach. By all the rules of the game a crash belly-landing with wheels up was the most that could be hoped for, but the captain was a gambler. 'Wheels, flaps, hold her steady, there's not all that much room, but I guess it will do,' and he put her down.

She ran to a stop with fifty yards to spare; no brakes, as the surface was an unknown quantity. 'What place is this – where do you calculate we are, Dave?' Dave the navigator hadn't a clue, and the fog closed in again as they paced out the area. They did not know if they were in Canada or Greenland! It was a smooth, hard-topped glacial moraine of about eleven hundred yards, running WNW by ESE. Sand and glaciated granite on clay gave a lovely hard surface.

There was no sign of life, so they all climbed back into the aircraft, drank the last dregs of coffee from their thermoses and went to sleep. Next day they tried to get the radio working but could not make contact, so they put in fifteen minutes on the key at the end of each hour just in case, ate some tinned fish, vomited it up and lay down in their blankets. Next day was much the same, but the batteries were getting weaker and they didn't expect to be heard. Then we came along in the Catalina.

After taking out guns, ammo and all movable equipment, the pilot took off next day with a skeleton crew and flew to BW8, where we were.

When I think of that grim Greenland coast and the fantastic improbability of the whole story, I wonder if fate had some great destiny for that Fortress crew, or are they just living quietly somewhere in the USA, now grandfathers, selling petrol or raising cattle?

That freak moraine is now marked on all the flying maps of Greenland and I shall never forget the moment when I first saw it.

Footnote: Bernt Balchen first gained fame as the pilot who rescued polar explorer Amundsen from Spitzbergen in 1925, and later flew over the North Pole.

In 1927 he was pilot of the Hudson Bay relief expedition and later became Chief Pilot to Byrd's Antarctic expedition, when he flew over the South Pole. Eventually he logged more hours over snow and ice than any other airman, and was known as a supremely skilful pilot. In 1948 he took charge of the American air base at Anchorage, Alaska. Later he became overall Director of Installations.

Not many who read this will have flown for long periods over snow, but I recall the feeling that I was flying in a bowl of milk, with sky and snow merging to give no apparent horizon, and no land features to give any perception of distance or height above surface.

18

Flying around Iceland – 1943

In March 1941 landing in Iceland meant coming back from a four-and-a-half-hour patrol well out to sea in a Battle, making for Kaldadarnes and landing on a short cocomatting and steel-mesh strip. There were no possibilities of diversion and the only radio aid was a rather doubtful QDM from the station HF/DF. If the wind didn't fit the runway, the old Battle was good at cross-wind landings. The 'Met' people did their best, but their information was scanty and their charts necessarily a compound of imagination and faith, backed by experience and patient study.

What a change two years had seen! Now Iceland had every facility, including well-organized flying control. With the absence of barrage balloons and the lack of blackout restrictions, landing in Iceland was now a better proposition than landing in many parts of the United Kingdom. The geographical features of Iceland were so pronounced that even a map on a 1/1,000,000 scale gave almost all the details one needed. The island itself was so large that even P/O Prune, flying from the United Kingdom, couldn't miss it altogether. Having made a landfall he would then have found it easy to crawl along the south coast, which had no fjords or deep indentations.

The first flight along the south coast of Iceland was an

unforgettable experience, and although duty more often demanded a landfall dead on track to Reykjavik, a course set for a point about forty miles west of Hofn took only a few minutes longer, and these could perhpas be written down to 'familiarisation'. Vatnajokull, the enormous ice-cap which reached to within a few hundred yards of the sea, was quite unmistakable. One glacier flowing out of Vatna came almost to the coast before ending abruptly in the shape of a lion's paw. At its extremity this was deeply crevassed, and reflected light sprang up from the depths of the paw, giving a deep sapphire glow. It must be a trick of light similar to the well-known 'daylight' signs used in advertising. The poet writes of 'Ice mast-high . . . as green as emerald', but in many hours flying over ice I have only once seen a green berg and never a green glacier.

Following the coastline to the west, one passed by mile after mile of flat, glacial moraine, intersected by ice-cold streams draining from the inland ice-caps; still further west were huge areas of black lava dust, formed by volcanic action at the end of the eighteenth century. Before this catastrophe, rich pasture land along the south coast had supported many thousands of sheep and cattle. At the southern-most point of Iceland, the black coastal desert ended abruptly in the craggy headlands of Portland and Vik; there was a small village here, and a camp with a radio station up on the hill.

Further to the west the friendly Westman Isles would be picked up in the summer months, more often than not from thirty to forty miles away. Heimaey, the largest isle, was an extinct volcano which had been cut in two as if smitten by some gigantic sword, and half the crater was now the harbour of a prosperous little fishing town. Gulls nested here in very large numbers. There were usually clusters of small fishing vessels tossing about in seas which were often very heavy.

From here onwards a little gentle map-reading brought one to the mouth of the Olfuss river, and to Kaldadarnes, cuddled into the river's lower elbow. Whether briefed to land here or not, it would not be a waste of time to look at Kaldadarnes, as it was on the way anyhow. The immediate approaches were good, and the high ground to the north and west was several miles away.

If there was no low cloud, it was usual to cut across country just west of Kaldadarnes. Reykjavik was then only ten minutes away. If this was not possible, more coast-crawling had to be done until the low ground to the east of Grindavik was reached, when it was usually possible to cut across the isthmus. If there was much low cloud this was a bad thing to do, as there were several rather unusual volcanic hills rising very suddenly just where you would least expect them. One of these hills reminded me of a gigantic rubbish dump, or ash-heap, which in point of fact it was, thrown up from nature's industrial regions just below. In shape it was a perfect cone and quite unmistakable. A Sunderland and an American PBY had crashed in this area while taking a short cut in poor weather.

There were many hot springs here and their plumes of steam began to suggest the direction of landing, now only a few minutes away. Across the peninsular the west coast was picked up and followed up to Hafnarfjordur, a medium-sized fishing town with a small harbour and quays. Hafnarfjordur past, and Reykjavik in sight, the course would normally pass over the country house of the Regent of Iceland, Mr Sven Bjornson, a house conspicuous for its clean white walls and tiny spired chapel. There was a lot of traffic around Reykjavik then, and on a fine day you would probably have to join the circle of aircraft milling around waiting for a 'green'. The circuit took you over the harbour, usually full of merchant ships; they were well trained and never shot at aircraft coming in to land those days. The cathedral stood on the highest point of the town, which it seemed to dominate, with its steep, rock-like proportions. The wind was usually south-westerly, and the approach lay over the harbour and town; the Hotel Borg and the post office, on opposite sides of the main square, were seventy-eighty ft. high, but there was plenty of clearance, and those tall radio masts south of the town were well off to starboard. Lake, park, a few hundred yards of meadow and there was the runway. It sloped up for part of its length and then over and down in a gentle gradient, right to the sea. It was a good, wide runway. As you braked, you had to remember that two years before this airfield had been an undrained swamp, and that off the runways it still retained some of its old characteristics.

Coming from the States, or from a patrol out to the south-west, you could afford to make a landfall anywhere and coast-crawl. The west coast was not quite so friendly as the south. By far the best landmark on the west coast was Snaefellsjokul, which loomed up like a piece of grounded cumulus stuck on to a mountain. Often it could be picked up more than eighty miles away. It then provided an unusually good visual running fix. I once found it very useful coming in from the west with W/T US and flying over 10/10 st.cu. up to 2,500 feet – it stuck up like a Persil-washed pillow from the dingier counterpane of rippled cloud, and was first recognised over fifty miles away. When breaking cloud off south-west Iceland, you had to remember the Fuglasker, those tiny bird-sanctuary islands ten or twenty miles south-west of Rekjanes; one of them was 226 feet high and looked very hard.

If the weather was really bad and no radical diversion was possible, there was a north-south strip of excellent rolled turf at Skagi, right on the tip of the Keflavik peninsular. This emergency landing-ground was only a few yards from the coast and practically at sea level. A glance at the map showed that this strip cannot be mistaken. An added advantage was the presence close by of the RAF D/F station at Sandgerdi, noted for its most reliable bearings. These signal airmen were very versatile, and would speedily lay out a flarepath at night. Incidentally, they usually had plenty of fresh eggs there – these were scarce in Reykjavik. There were two American airfields near Keflavik, in the south of this peninsular, known as Meeks and Patterson Fields.

All towns and villages in Iceland were lit up at night and, to a war-weary traveller from England, Reykjavik then looked like fairy-land. Most of the lighthouses along the coast were still lit; you should have been briefed with their characteristics.

So far no mention has been made of wireless aids, but Iceland offered plenty of these. In addition to the normal types of RAF, HF and MF stations, there was an American 'Radio Range' about a mile south of Reykjavik, and three Icelandic trawler beacons along the south coast. The most powerful station in the whole of Iceland was the civil broadcasting station, capable of pushing out 100 kw. on 271 kc/s although it normally worked on much lower power. This had been found reliable up to 500 miles away and more than one pilot had homed with his loop all the way to Iceland from Northern Ireland.

The Intelligence Officer at the airfield of departure would normally have been able to provide the hours of transmission.

Space does not permit a thorough survey of all airfields and emergency landing-grounds in Iceland, but a few minutes spent before take-off, marking in emergency landing grounds (ELGs) on a flying map, would not have been wasted. Along the south coast there were many stretches of sand where a belly-landing could have been safely made, and some good enough for a normal landing. If you had to try this, you had to look out for the Icelandic telephone line which linked up the coastal villages; a certain Group Captain once made an inverted landing in a Moth just south of Kaldadarnes while sabotaging this line.

Nothing has yet been said of flying boats, but nature had provided many sheltered bays and fjords where they could put down, and there were no very strong currents around Iceland. Mooring buoys existed only at Skerjafjordur (Reykjavik), Akureyri (in the north) and Budareyri (in the east). The last-named base had been used only for Northrop seaplanes and the fjord was too narrow to be safe for large flying boats except in very good weather.

In the early days, the spirit of adventure prompted one Battle pilot to land on Vatnajokul; that he took off again without incident demonstrates the fact that most ice-caps of any size are smooth and flat towards their centres. In the autumn of 1940, a flight commander of 98, the first squadron in Iceland, forced-landed on this same ice-cap with the British Army G–1 as passenger. They reached a farm after two days' tramping and were picked up safely by the search party. Ice-caps are not, however, recommended as ELGs.

Although in winter we had our share of darkness, for many weeks in summer there was perpetual daylight, an advantage which all the ingenuity of Flying Control could not achieve in the United Kingdom. Yes, landing in Iceland in 1943 was a piece of cake.

Glossary

QDM	=	magnetic course to steer (for base).
HF D/F	=	high-frequency direction finding.

P/O Prune	=	mythical junior RAF officer, prone to errors.
Heimaey	=	called an 'extinct' volcano. Erupted violently a few years ago.
W/T US	=	radio unserviceable.
st.cu.	=	strato-cumulus cloud.
Radio Range	=	homing radio beams.
Moth	=	Tiger Moth, single-engined biplane used for training and practice in 'real flying'.
Army G–1	=	Chief Staff Officer, operational.

19

With a convoy to Russia

During the Second World War there were standing arrangements for RAF aircrew to spend a short time afloat with the Royal Navy, as well as for sea-going naval officers to fly with Coastal Command; both sides gained a lot from the plan. This story, however, deals with the day-to-day experiences (leaving out enemy action) of twelve officers and 120 NCOs and men taking passage to north Russia via a 'County'-class cruiser (HMS *Cumberland*, Capt. A. H. Maxwell-Hyslop, RN) and starts on a cold Sunday morning in Loch Ewe, on the west coast of Scotland. As the tender drew away from the quayside a very young pilot officer stood aloof, with a resigned expression on his white, drawn face; he thought the whole voyage to Murmansk was being made on the small tender!

WITH A CONVOY TO RUSSIA

Twenty minutes later, all were aboard the cruiser, sitting down to their best Sunday dinner for months. The date was February 1943.

We were the advance party of 30 Wing, planned to operate from Murmansk, Vaenga and Lake Lakta to provide air cover for our fortnightly Russian convoys. In the event, Moscow refused to cooperate and our stay was short-lived, to the embarrassment of local Russian forces in Kola Inlet.

Putting up over a hundred airmen in a fighting ship must have been a problem. A Walrus aircraft was turned out of its hangar to give space for over fifty and most of the rest were put in the fore cabin flat. Senior NCOs took over the Petty Officers' recreation room and officers slept in the bathroom flats and in the wardroom. The men were not very keen on hammocks at first, but quickly came to prefer them. As senior RAF officer, I had the Navigating Officer's day cabin, abaft 'B' turret, with my own steward (a marine).

A few hours after sailing, the ship ran into a gale which blew – for several days; the RAF and not a few of the Navy were thoroughly and miserably sick. In our innocence we thought this weather was normal, but an old CPO told me confidentially that in his thirty years of service he had never known it quite so bad, and this helped. Waves were so huge that a destroyer less than a mile away was hidden from view one moment and high on a crest the next. At least we were free from any fear of U-boats in conditions like that, as no torpedo could run through such waves and troughs. Later on we heard that the weather alone had sunk one freighter, smashed the bows of a small aircraft carrier, HMS *Dasher*, and jammed the turret of a light cruiser (HMS *Sheffield*), all in our convoy, forcing them back to the Clyde for repairs.

Perhaps the criterion of seasickness is this: can you, while being sick yourself, still laugh at someone in the same plight?

If you can, then there is still hope. I stopped laughing on the second day out and for another thirty-six hours did not care if I lived or died. The Naval Commander belonged to the tough school of 'Bring 'em out on deck and the fresh air will put them right', but fortunately the sea was too rough for this. There seemed to be only one real cure: to be sick for forty-eight hours and tire out the reflexes. Of course, if a voyage is to last only two days this philosophy has little practical value, but over a fortnight it proved to be true. After the second day everyone recovered and thereafter came through even rougher weather unscathed. Incidentally, the PMO at Coastal Command HQ had given me, for us all, some white tablets, said to be the latest thing in medicine to prevent seasickness. Had he been aboard he would have heard many suggestions as to what he could do with his white tablets!

The second blow to our prestige was the rum ration débâcle: eighty-eight airmen put their names down for the daily tot at 'Up Spirits', but only nine could take it and, according to ancient custom, the other seventy-nine tots were ditched over the side, amid groans from the petty officers and older naval hands. This was the deepest humiliation of all, but I negotiated a revised list of only a dozen rum-drinkers and these gave no further cause for complaint. From memory, I think non-drinkers received threepence (in old currency) a day in lieu. Sea-legs acquired, all began to shake down and find their way about the ship. Port and starboard, forrard and aft began to mean something and it became quite natural to call the enclosed deck space 'flats' and the toilets 'heads'.

We were all given Action Stations and exercised at dawn every day. Some were lucky and had Oerlikons and Brens to man, others were on damage control and ammunition parties. As a presumed expert on enemy aircraft identification I was on the ADP gallery above the bridge and suffered the latter's wind deflection, which gave me and two seamen their breeze as well as our own.

The first time the klaxon went for a real alarm, we were at tea and, being keen types, left mugs, knives and forks, etc., as we ran to Action Stations. A good many deficiencies in seamen's kits were made up that afternoon; experience is a hard school! The next day the alarm went while four of us were being shown over one of the magazines in the bowels of the ship and the sub. taking us round said quietly, 'You must hurry, we always flood the magazines in action.' Several knuckles were barked in the scramble before we caught on . . .

The voyage was broken after a few days by a call in Seydisfjord, on the east coast of Iceland, entered in a snow-storm after two days hove-to outside. At least I was on familiar ground, having served eighteen months in Iceland just prior to this trip. The captain retired from the bridge, where he lived at sea, to his more spacious quarters aft and in deference to his need for rest, no one trod on the after portion of the quarterdeck. When he did appear on deck, all officers at once crossed to port, leaving the starboard side clear for him. Usually he called the senior officer present to walk up and down with him. I was so honoured several times.

A day or two in the calm waters of the fjord allowed AA target practice on a towed target. An unfortunate burst of fire ahead of the plane brought a rude signal from the very junior Fleet Air Arm pilot: 'Hi, I'm towing this drogue, not pushing it!'

When the American half of our convoy had joined us (making thirty-five merchant ships in all) we sailed for Kola Inlet, north Russia, and the very next day had a long-range Focke Wulf Condor shadowing us at a safe distance. How we missed that Woolworth Carrier, with its fighter aircraft, being repaired in the Clyde! Round and round he went, just out of gun range. 'Guns' tried an eight-inch on him, but no luck. The story went that on a previous convoy lamp signals had been exchanged thus:

'Please go round the other way, you make us dizzy.'
'Anything to oblige, Englishman,' followed by a reversal of direction.

Anyway, an RAF corporal on look-out saw the enemy aircraft first, which was very right and proper and helped to restore some of our self-respect.

The naval system of 'piping' orders seemed strange at first, but after the first week appeared perfectly logical. All naval orders were announced over the ship's loudspeakers and preceded by a few notes on a shrill whistle; some of the more important were also preceded by a bugle call. Nelson did not have loudspeakers but otherwise used the same system.

Very early in the morning, a bugle sounded, then the pipe shrilled and a stentorian voice called, 'A-a-all hands! 'Eavow– 'eavow– 'eavow– 'eavow, lash up and stow!' A little later the pipe went again, with, 'All hands to Action Stations!' and when or if dawn broke with no trouble, all stood down except the Duty Watch. After a while, the ear became attuned to the note of the pipe and subconsciously it got sorted out from the din and bustle of the ship and demanded attention. Piping a distinguished officer on board was itself an interesting process for the Air Force to watch, but the spectacle of an admiral being piped over the side as he flew off in a catapulted Walrus was strange indeed.

During that part of the voyage nearest to enemy territory (occupied Norway) all hands were closed up at Action Stations for long periods, but even then hot food was taken round every two hours. Pails of steaming soup, 'titti-oggies' (naval cornish pasties) and 'ki' (very thick, hot cocoa). At times like these, pursers had their uses.

My clearest memories of these long spells at Action Stations include: admiration for the speed of training and elevating the big eight-inch guns; sympathy for the men on the 'B' turret Oerlikon (exposed to everything while running into a storm at twenty-two knots in twenty degrees of frost), and the ease with which one could sleep on a bare steel deck when really tired.

In the wardroom all the specialist officers, like the dwarfs in *Snow White*, were suitably nicknamed: 'Guns', 'Schoolie', 'Doc', 'Toothy' are obvious; the engineers were 'Plumbers'. In addition, the Commander(E) was called the Chief Engineer and his second-in-command just 'Senior'. The senior officer of the Royal Marines was 'Major', although he was only a captain. The Paymaster Commander was 'Pay' and the Navigation Officer 'Pilot' ('Pontius' to some!). 'Torps' was in charge of torpedo tubes and all electrical installations. 'Number One' and over him 'the Commander' were the two executive officers responsible to the captain for the running of the ship.

The ship's loudspeaker system was used for talks, quiz contests and brains trusts, and for broadcasting impromptu concerts. For the record, we were unbeaten at quizzes and also played a part in several concerts. The captain spoke as soon as the ship had sailed and explained the purpose of the voyage and when we expected to arrive; almost every day the commander used to broadcast an appreciation of the situation and discuss alterations in routine and prospects of action. While we were on this trip the Germans appointed Doenitz as Senior Admiral and the captain broadcast this titbit, with the comment that this was likely to increase our 'hope' of bringing the enemy to action. As the enemy consisted of 'pocket battleships' with eleven-inch guns, as well as the mighty *Tirpitz*, we did not all share this 'hope'.

As senior RAF officer aboard, I was several times honoured by invitations to dine with the captain, who normally dined alone. During one of these pleasant occasions I remember him explaining that his tactic would be to steam at full speed towards the enemy to close the range to within that of our own eight-inch guns, should we have the good fortune to encounter the *Tirpitz*, etc.

Incidentally, when somewhere in the vicinity of Bear Island we intercepted a signal from C.-in-C. HF: 'Request gate Scapa 0700'. The Home Fleet was too important to risk north of 70°N at this stage of the war, but this did give us a feeling of being rather lonely. Our battle fleet was normally somewhere out to the west of us, ready to engage any major German warships should they emerge from anchorage in Norwegian fjords. From now on we really were on our own.

Apart from the broadcasts already mentioned, there were occasional cinema shows and almost every day a half-hour talk on some topic. I spoke on the work of Coastal Command, and on Iceland. Senior spoke of his spell in a French prisoner-of-war camp in Dakar and so on. On Sunday came 'Divisions', when each officer paraded his men for the captain's inspection, followed by church parade, with the captain reading the lessons. The improvised ship's chapel was crowded with men taking holy communion, and the ship's padre was in great demand.

The ship's company was divided into four watches: first port, second port, first starboard and second starboard. This had no connection with duties on one side of the ship or the other and as far as I could see the watches might just as well have been called A, B, C and D.

When Action Stations sounded, all four watches were closed

up simultaneously, resulting in the overcrowding of some stations, but no doubt there were good reasons for this. Normally only one watch was on at a time.

To keep as far as possible from the enemy coast (not very far, at that) we kept close to the edge of the pack ice north of Bear Island. Here the sea-water was on the point of freezing and did so when the bows crashed through waves and the spray hit the superstructure. This extra top weight was very dangerous and could have made us capsize unless removed, so day after day there was the finger-numbing routine of chipping ice off masts, stays, decks, etc. A nice job that was. We did have special clothing for these Arctic duties and no signs of rank were visible. As Squadron Leader i/c I remember being relieved by an AC2 with the formula (acquired from the naval ratings?): 'You can flick off now, mate.' I then realized why the Commander had his rank painted on the back of his parka. In the end we got to Murmansk with most of our ships, but still found no peace, as we were attacked by aircraft even in the last few miles down Kola Inlet. By that time we knew much more about the Navy and had also arrived at our new station.

P.S. Out of the blue in February 1992 came a Russian campaign Medal (1941/45), exactly fifty years after the events just described.

Glossary

'County'-class cruiser	– heavy cruiser carrying 8-inch calibre guns.
Walrus	– small amphibian aircraft later used mostly for air/sea rescue work around Britain.
CPO	– Chief Petty Officer, equivalent to

	Army Sergeant-Major.
PMO	– Principal Medical Officer.
Oerlikons and Brens	– light anti-aircraft guns.
ADP	– Air Defence Position.
Sub.	– Sub-lieutenant (junior naval officer).
C.-in-C. HF	– Commander-in-Chief, Home Fleet.
'Request Gate Scapa'	– asking for the anti-submarine boom defending Scapa Flow anchorage (Orkney Isles) to be opened to allow the fleet to enter.
AC2	– Aircraftman Second Class, equivalent to a private soldier in the Army.

Mediterranean 1943–1945

20

Fun at Gibraltar

Stationed at Gibraltar in 1944 was a very brave, popular and universally respected destroyer captain, Lt. Cdr Smallwood, RN, also well known in UK rugger circles. There were occasionally some very quiet periods in the war, livened up by parties from time to time. After one such aboard his destroyer, John Smallwood decided that his ship's company needed some practice in dealing with an emergency, so at about 0100 hours he called for 'Action Stations' to repel boarders. In order to make this more realistic, his crew were given small-arms practice against boats thought to be approaching his ship with hostile intent. The crackle of small-arms fire and the sight of tracer rounds flying about the harbour in the small hours of an otherwise quiet night aroused some interest, even alarm. However, verbal explanations by loud-hailer were accepted, but the incident was, unfortunately, officially logged by the Port Officer of the Watch.

In those days, as Chief Intelligence Officer (RAF) I received a courtesy copy of all pink naval signals, delivered to my duty officer in the centre of the Rock, just opposite the naval cipher office, halfway along the Admiralty tunnel. Arriving there for duty at 0800 hours and flipping through the night's crop of signals, I spotted this report of small-arms fire in the harbour and made some enquiries. I then realised that FOGMA (Flag Officer Gibraltar and Mediterranean Approaches – Vice-Admiral Sir Harold Burrough) would be going through his file clip about an hour later, and would have to take some official action. His chief of staff (a senior captain and a most formidable character) would also see it, and the naval disciplinary machine would then order an enquiry. I contacted the senior WRN officer on duty (a good friend of mine) and we both felt that it was in the best interest of the service that Smallwood's good name should be protected. We extracted the offending signal from FOGMA's clip and destroyed it, along with all copies, and deleted all references in the signal log. Later in the morning I had a friendly chat with the Port Signals Officer (Lt. Cdr Sir Marshall Warmington Bt., RN), who agreed that it was in the best tradition of the service to follow Nelson's lead and put a blind eye to the telescope.

The subject was never mentioned again and, so far as I know, the admiral never found out. At least, he didn't get to know officially and that was the point. I only hope that, nearly fifty years later, I won't face a court-martial for what I did!

21

Grim coincidences

A vital part of the invasion of Sicily on 10 July 1943 (Operation 'Husky') was the air drop of parachute troops, carried by over a hundred Dakotas flying with full petrol tanks the eleven hundred miles from Gibraltar to Sicily. This involved a night take-off from North Front airstrip, and I retain a vivid memory of these aircraft taking off in rapid succession from east to west, with front wing-lights giving the impression of cars on a main road.

After more than half of them were safely away, one aircraft, about a third of the way down the runway, veered off to the left and seemed to be heading directly for the air control tower, on the 'Rock' side of North Front. We expected a quick correction with no great trouble, as the runway was 150 yards wide, with extra tarmac space alongside. But on it came, and with it a realization that within a few seconds it would strike the tower. Three of us jumped from the gallery, and with sprained ankles scrambled a few yards before the Dakota (then almost airborne) struck and erupted into a ball of fire. The intense heat made it impossible to get anywhere near the crash and there was nothing we could do to help. The roar of the flames, the crackle of exploding ammunition, and the horrible smell of burning flesh, were like a medieval impression of Hell. Worst of all, a fully equipped and manned fire-tender and ambulance were parked alongside and went up in flames with the aircraft. This was a possibility which had clearly not been envisaged but, with the wisdom of hindsight, an Air Ministry order (AMO) was rapidly circulated from London specifically forbidding fire tenders and ambulances to be stationed either next to each other or alongside flying control towers. I expect that this is still in force today.

I was reminded of a somewhat similar incident, happily only affecting three crew and not fatal. This was at RAF Lee-on-Solent when I was stationed there in 1938. In those peaceful days the siren went at twelve noon on Saturdays and was the signal for everyone to rush happily home or to their RAF mess. At this precise moment, a Walrus amphibian aircraft, returning from a short flight round the Isle of Wight, crashed at the end of the short runway; everyone thought the emergency alarm was the normal noon signal and valuable minutes were lost before rescue work began.

An AMO rapidly amended the alarm drill. Not long after this, the Royal Navy took over and Lee became a 'stone frigate'. I have often wondered if they also took over our new procedure. We cannot always anticipate events, but at least we can (and did) learn from bitter experience.

22

Consol-navigation system

During 1944, military intelligence colleagues at Gibraltar began to receive reports from agents in Spain of Germans working on some kind of new radio station, first near Jerez, in the south, and later near Corunna, about 450 miles further north. Having a Photographic Reconnaissance Unit (PRU) of three Spitfires at North Front, we laid on flights at 19,000 feet-plus, with very long focal length fixed vertical cameras. At this height a Spitfire is virtually invisible and can only be spotted by radar, which the neutral Spanish did not have at that time. Our Photographic Interpretation Unit (PIU) soon spotted the common factor, which was a single tall mast, carrying something remarkably like a large cartwheel with spokes, mounted horizontally. All the usual signs of current work in progress were also clearly visible, i.e. new buildings, worn tracks and so on. All this meant nothing to me or to our Chief Signals Officer, but was readily understood at Air Ministry in England because, I believe, a similar station had been observed in occupied Norway.

Our first bonus was what we used to call 'diplomatic leverage'. We at Gibraltar enjoyed excellent relations with the Spanish, both military and civil, and they were very sensitive to our suggestions that Spain was somewhat less neutral in allowing German military personnel (albeit posing as civilians) to build military installations, helping their war effort against us on neutral territory. When somewhat embarrassed Spanish officials tried to say that these new buildings were really aerial lighthouses, we reacted with simulated incredulity. In common language, they 'owed us a favour' and we made use of this in a number of ways. One of these was the uninterrupted progress through Spain, from the Pyrenees to Gibraltar, of escaped Allied prisoners-of-war. On one occasion, a party of six came through on a temporary Spanish visa as 'theological students'. Any people less like theological students I had never seen, and I am sure the Spanish authorities knew this as well as we did. We always emphasised our traditional friendship, going back to the Napoleonic Wars. An interesting survival, useful in our work, were the estates in Spain given to Sir Arthur Wellesley (later Duke of Wellington) in recognition of his leadership and success in the war against the French 150 years earlier. Although not really part of this story, it happened that Captain the Duke of Wellington was stationed in Gibraltar for a short time. I knew him quite well and also remember, while having a drink with him, introducing him to a brigadier bridge-playing friend, who thought I was pulling his leg! Sadly, the Duke was killed in action in Greece a few months later.

With remarkable speed, our colleagues in Britain produced and printed what were known as 'Consol' navigation charts, with a pattern of intersecting hyperbolae based on the geographical pin-points which we had supplied. By the time the German radio stations began to transmit, we already had these charts available for use by our aircraft on operations or in transit off the Bay of Biscay and the west coast of Spain and Portugal. The Consol stations were, of course, designed to aid U-boat navigation, but were even more useful to us than to our enemies. They were very simple to use, needing only a simple radio receiver tuned to the known frequencies of Jerez and Corunna, and the ability to count up to forty-nine! Both stations radiated a repeating pattern of dots and dashes, 'dits' and 'dahs', adding up to forty-nine. The pattern or ratio of 'dits' to 'dahs', e.g. 21:28, determined the curve on which the signal was being received. The pattern from the twin Consol station gave a second curve, and where the two curves intersected was a fairly accurate position for aircraft or U-boat.

How did it work? It was based on the speed of travel of radio waves, the same as that of light, 186,000 miles a second. Expressed in micro-seconds (MS or one-millionth secs), this becomes 0.186 miles per MS, or 18.6 miles (30 km.) per 100 MS. As the curves were 30 km. apart on the charts, all the radio receiver had to do was to measure signals spaced 100 micro-seconds apart and record these in terms of dots and dashes. After the war, this system of navigation (with sixty 'dits' and 'dahs' more accurately replacing the original forty-nine) was in common use for over forty years, but has now been superseded by satellite radio stations in earth orbit.

23

Foss Way – Gibraltar

The Rock of Gibraltar has been part of our history for many generations, and once again, in the Second World War, it played a unique part as our sole foothold on the European continent, not only dominating the entrance to the Mediterranean, as in Nelson's time, but with a completely new role as a strategic air base and staging-post for aircraft. Once again, fresh tunnels were cut into and through that massive block of Jurassic limestone. A modern aircraft runway over a mile long and twice normal width was built from excavated material, over the old garrison racecourse at North Front and well out to sea. Squadrons of Catalina and Sunderland flying boats joined warships in an extension to the harbour at New Quay. A mooring mast for airships (of the US Navy) was also built at Europa Point.

Naturally, building tunnels and key facilities in solid rock is a specialized task needing unusual skills, and these were provided by tunnelling units of the Royal Engineers, largely recruited from mining engineers and geologists with experience from all over the world. It came about that there was a close affinity between aircrews of the RAF and tunnellers of the RE, which provides the substance of this particular story.

Oddly enough, both mining engineers prospecting and working for minerals, and navigators of Coastal Command need to know exactly where they are on the surface of the earth, often when there are no recognisable landmarks for hundreds of miles. Both use astro-navigation, involving specialized equipment and skills in identifying specific stars, measuring their altitudes at times correct to a second or two and so on. I well remember the interest and delight shown by Air Marshal Sir Philip Joubert, C.-in-C. Coastal Command, on one of his visits, when I told him that the tunnellers were teaching the RAF how to navigate! His first question was, 'And what are the RAF teaching the tunnellers?' One answer to this was that we took them flying, perhaps the perfect change of scene from working hundreds of feet underground.

It was during this period that by chance the tunnellers

broke into a huge new cave, deep in the Rock, with stalactites, a large lake of fresh water and a curious ledge around it at water level, projecting from the vertical cave wall. This was a form of lateral stalactite formed over thousands of years by water slowly evaporating at constant level. It was just possible to walk around the cave on this natural ledge, though with great difficulty. There was already a well-known system of small caves, known as St Michael's Caves, but this was an unconnected and entirely separate one. I had the pleasure of being almost the first non-tunneller to see it when they telephoned me to come and have a look. Except for hand torches, it was then in complete darkness, of course, but what impressed me most was the absolute silence of the place. Later on it was wired up for lighting and for a time became a favourite site to show visiting VIPs, but after a while it was closed because there were plans to use the water as an additional reservoir for human consumption.

A great friend at that time was Major Foss, a Canadian mining engineer in command of the tunnellers. He was very keen to see some action against the enemy, so it was arranged that he fly on a night sortie against U-boats, and since no passengers were taken on such trips he acted as front gunner in a Leigh Light Wellington of 279 Squadron (*see* Chapter 26). On his first trip he had the great satisfaction of finding and attacking an enemy submarine cruising on the surface and charging its batteries in the (supposed!) safety of darkness, about 300 miles east of Gibraltar in the Mediterranean. I can still remember him bursting into my office, deep in the Rock, about 09.00 hrs that morning to tell me all about it. He was like a youngster, flushed with delight and excitement and pouring out his story. He had been manning a single gun in the nose as they came in to illuminate a radar target on the surface, and for once it was not the usual Spanish tunny-fishing boat, but the real thing. He opened fire and saw sparks from his tracer rounds bouncing off the conning tower and hull; in fact, he fired in one long continuous burst and his gun jammed through over-heating, but it was all over in a few seconds as they gained height to get away from the exploding depth-charges. I took notes of his story to supplement the official report, which had already arrived by teleprinter from North Front, and told him to have a good breakfast and then get his head down. We agreed to meet for a drink that evening. Alas, my phone rang three or four hours later to say that his batman had found him dead, lying in a chair at his quarters, with a happy smile on his face. My emotions were very, very mixed. I had lost a close friend and perhaps it was my fault for helping him to get on this flight, but he had been a fit man and very keen to go. We gave him full military honours, with a sizeable RAF party slow-marching in the cortège. Shortly afterwards, the main new tunnel in the Rock was named Foss Way in his honour, apt in more than one respect. Sad though it was at the time, he died a happy man, and if he had an unsuspected heart condition it could have happened anyway, as an RAF medical officer, a mutual friend, explained to me.

Almost twenty years later, in the Northern Rhodesian copperbelt of central Africa, I was having dinner with the Canadian manager of a big copper mine and the conversation turned to the war. I must have mentioned Gibraltar, I suppose, because I was asked if I had ever come across a Major Foss, an old friend of his who had died there. I was able to give him a complete account and gathered that the family had been told only that he died 'on active service' (the routine alternative to 'killed in action') in Gibraltar on a certain date. I subsequently learned how much his family and friends had appreciated the full story, with the background of our RAF/

tunneller friendship. I feel that 'killed in action' might have been the more accurate description in his case.

As a postscript, the U-boat, severely damaged, managed to limp back to base in the south of France but was out of action for a long time.

24

No balloons for the Admiral

In the spring of 1944 the Mediterranean Sea was open and convoys laden with tanks, guns and stores no longer had to travel thousands of miles all around Africa to get to the troops in southern Italy and the north African coast. The enemy was quick to appreciate how much easier it was to eliminate fifty tanks by sinking a ship than by knocking them out one by one on the battlefield, and moved squadrons of Ju 88s and Heinkel torpedo-bombers to airfields at Salon, Istre, Montpelier and Perpignan in the south of France to attack our convoys in the western Med. as they hugged the north African coast.

'Gerry, look at this signal: three more ships torpedoed at dusk last night, that's another 150 tanks gone to the bottom. I don't know how they find these convoys so regularly. Yes, I know their agents always spot them going through the Strait here, it's only twelve miles wide anyway and we can't stop that; but three years ago we were trying the same game with enemy ships off Norway without much success and we had radar (ASV, as we called it then).'

There were lots of things to do and the main job of the RAF in Gibraltar was to hunt U-boats and escort convoys in the Atlantic. We knew many of the sea-going officers, however, and I regularly briefed them on the enemy air situation and how best to deal with it. It was interesting to have a drink with naval officers from the escort group based on Gibraltar and hear about the attacks at first hand.

'Yes, John, I know you had been shadowed during the day but was there an aircraft with you just before dusk? Definitely not, you say? Well how do you accout for them finding you in light mist at dusk? You say two or three aircraft found you first and these were overhead, dropping flares; did you fire at them?' 'I'll say we did – they were dropping bombs around the place. What do you expect us to do? Then the torpedo bombers appeared unexpectedly from the dark horizon and in a moment there seemed to be torpedo tracks everywhere. Five merchantmen were hit and three sank within minutes. We got in some shots but they turned away and didn't fly over us.'

It looked very much as if the enemy recce planes had some special device for finding the convoys at dusk, and then marked them with flares. Tracer going up vertically at the flares and recce aircraft only confirmed the accuracy of their placement, and acted as guiding beacons to the torpedo aircraft coming up a few miles away a few feet above the waves. Then came a stroke of luck and a ship bound for Gibraltar picked up survivors from a German aircraft which had crashed into the sea after being damaged by gunfire. 'Herr Leutnant, you speak very good English. For you the war is over and I congratulate you.' 'Yes, my Squadron Leader, I was for many years in England with radio works. First we must finish Russia and then you will see, all will be over very soon and then we are friends again, eh?'

'Herr Wulman, you should be with us still, working on radio, we have some wonderful apparatus now for finding targets at night. It is lucky for us you have not radar.' 'My dear Squadron Leader, how do you think we can find your convoys at night? You cannot stop it so I can tell you: we too have radar, and soon we shall have it much better than you.'

One thing still puzzled me. Granted that the enemy had radar, I would have expected the 'blip' from the actual coastline to have masked the echo from the ships, as they were scarcely a mile offshore when attacked. I spoke to our radar officer, a young Canadian, about this and he agreed, except that if the coastline was rather flat and the ships had tall masts they might show up more clearly at a distance. 'What about 400 feet of steel cable?' 'I guess you are joking, Prof, why would ships want to help by putting up a radar beacon? No, I haven't seen ships with balloons on them and don't believe it anyway.'

An old friend pitched up in Gibraltar next day. This was one of the interesting things about that place, it was a sort of wartime Piccadilly Circus and almost everyone came through sooner or later.

'Hello, Steve, what on earth are you doing in Gibraltar – I thought you were running the war from Shepheards? Leave! You lucky chap, join us for a spot at the Rock, it's nearly lunchtime anyway. When did you get in?' 'Last night, in a Dak. We flew along the coast from Maison Blanche. If you're still in Coastal, Prof, you might be interested in this one. Off Tenes we saw a funny sight. A bit of low mist, with dusk coming on – cold air off the coast, probably – and there sticking up like Belisha beacons were half a dozen barrage balloons, just like good old London Town.

'A convoy, I suppose, but we couldn't see any ships. Just as well we were friendly, with a clear sky and a fat moon coming up fast, we could have done some lovely bombing on them.'

Another eastbound convoy was due to pass through the Strait that night and in the afternoon my friends from the Escort Group looked in. 'Well, Prof, have you any air cover for us this time? The Army needs those tanks, you know.'

'Sorry, Tom, no can do. Look at this map. The enemy never attacks until you're past Oran and he comes in at dusk, as you know. We have no Fighter Control along this coast and won't have for several months. Fighters stooging around blind wouldn't help you at all. We can give you a bit more gen this time, though. If they drop flares above you I want you to fire a red signal flare into the middle of them. We think the enemy commander controls the whole operation sitting 10,000 feet up and OK's the flares by a green and cancels them with a red. If a red appears the enemy pilots have orders to ignore those flares as being wrongly placed, so could you have an escort standing off a mile or two and get her to put up starshell and a green? Fine. And please don't fire at the odd aircraft high up. No, they won't be friendly, I know, in fact they may drop a bomb or two, but the chance of damage will be very small, as they will be looking at their own flares hanging in the sky between you and them.

'The damage is done when you open fire; your vertical tracer fire gives the torpedo aircraft a perfect "come-in" beacon and aiming mark. Could you get your gunners not even to look at the flares – it takes a minute or two to get night vision back and the real danger is coming low down from the dark horizon, remember. Keep your guns trained on this area and explain to your guncrews that they must keep their night vision. Give 'em lots of carrots! Oh, and do you have to fly balloons? They don't help, you know, and we think the enemy planes, or one or two of them anyway, have radar and get a good echo from the cables.' 'Thanks, Prof, you certainly tell a good story, but Fleet Orders say that AA balloons will be streamed by convoys in the western Med.' 'Why not follow Nelson's example and turn a blind eye to the order about balloons? You could fly them going past your HQ and keep them down the rest of the time.'

'Well, yes, I suppose we could keep them close-hauled except when we pass in sight of Algiers (where C.-in-C. Med. had a villa high up on the hill). How about coming with us yourself anyway? You'd love to? That's fine, be our mascot in HMS *Pheasant* and we'll send you over in a boat to join a merchant ship detaching at Algiers and you can fly back.'

Such is the irony of war that all I had was a pleasant Mediterranean cruise for three or four days and we didn't see a darn thing. The last three convoys had been attacked (and so were the next four) but somehow this one was missed. My naval friends were undoubtedly sincere when they said I was welcome to come again any time!

I did at least have plenty of time to question the ship's company about every detail of the enemy attacks on previous convoys, and got all the information I needed, though unfortunately I failed to see an attack at first hand.

Oddly enough, I couldn't get back to Gibraltar at once; I had to have a certificate of vaccination not more than fourteen days old to get back, as there was quite a scare on about smallpox at the time. I found the Command MO to be an old friend, Jumbo Muir from Icelandic days, and we pondered on the changing ways of the medical profession. It used to be seven years, then three years and now I'd been vaccinated three weeks ago and had to be done again. The new rules said that no one would be allowed into Gibraltar without a certificate of vaccination – dated not more than fourteen days previously! I was 'done' and the extra evening in Algiers enabled me to look up American General Morris, another old friend from Reykjavik, now commanding all the American Air Force in north Africa and one of the finest bridge players in the service, I would say.

Back in Gibraltar there was plenty of work on hand and it didn't seem long before the next escort group came in for a briefing. The word seemed to have been passed around and they were more than ready to try the game with the red and green flares and have the balloons kept down. We followed the fortunes of this convoy with even more than the usual interest. They were picked up and shadowed by a couple of Ju 88s as usual, one after the other. Then a breathing space and we waited in the Ops. Room for nightfall and the naval pink signals which would tell the story. 'Escort vessel attacked by enemy aircraft position so-and-so. Estimate one aircraft damaged by gunfire.'

'Senior naval officer reports flares dropped overhead position so-and-so. Tracer from detached escort vessel seen bearing 085 degrees True, seven miles.' 'SNO reports no further enemy activity. Aircraft engines heard when detached escort attacked. No damage to escort or convoy.'

The following night the convoy was attacked, but only by bombers; no torpedoes. Only one ship was hit and by the following night, they were out of the normal attacking area. We looked forward keenly to the return of the escort and a firsthand account of it all but something else happened first.

A good C.-in-C. always knows what is going on, and Admiral Cunningham, on an official visit to Gibraltar, called for the Squadron Leader who was persuading the ships to disobey his orders. I was asked to dinner at the Mount and Admiral Sir Harold Burrough sat me next to the C.-in-C.

'Well, Brown, I want you to tell me about this balloon business. I believe ships are disregarding my orders and doing what you tell them.'

Admiral Cunningham, small, pleasant and quietly spoken, listened attentively as the case was put.

'Very well, Brown, I think I see the reason for this, but I'm not a signals man. I will send my signals officer to talk to you about it.' A couple of days later a tall Commander RN flew in to Gibraltar and we went into all the evidence available on these attacks and agreed that convoys in the western Med. should no longer fly balloons. Fleet Orders were amended and from then on balloons were kept close-hauled even when passing Algiers. A few weeks later the Strategic Air Force in the Med. was turned on to the airfields in the south of France and the Germans never afterwards showed quite the same enthusiasm for finding convoys. Within a few months the RAF had night-flying Beaufighter aircraft plus Ground-Controlled Interception Units along that coast. Tanks for the Eighth Army were now arriving safely.

25

'Met' flights and unusual cargoes

Today our planet is encircled by orbiting satellites sending back a continual stream of observations and photographs, from which we know exactly what the weather is almost everywhere on earth. Only a few years ago, the RAF had to gather its own weather data (barometric pressure, temperature at various heights), either by balloons or special flights. As a schoolboy in Cambridge in the 1920s I remember the daily vertical weather flights by a biplane fighter from RAF Duxford; on one occasion I was late for school because a weather plane had landed on the railway line near Fulbourn in dense fog. We understood that the pilot was committed to a high-altitude flight at dawn every day, however bad the weather was, and that after six months he automatically collected a well-deserved AFC (Air Force Cross) for distinguished flying.

Some twenty years later, we were at war and had regular flights by specially equipped Halifax aircraft flying hundreds of miles over the Atlantic in a SW direction from Lands End, taking readings of temperature and air pressure at various heights. This provided the additional information needed by meteorological officers drawing their eight-hourly synoptic charts from which aircrews were briefed before every flight. Put simply, most of our UK weather comes to us from the south-west, and so a look at the weather today 900 miles out over the Atlantic often tells us what weather we shall have tomorrow or the next day. In the last two years of the Second World War this work was done by a flight of 'Met' Halifaxes based at St Eval or St Mawgan, in Cornwall, and commanded by W/Cdr Paul Linham (whose wife lived next to mine in Old Hunstanton, from earlier days when we had both been stationed at Bircham Newton).

Sometimes weather conditions in Cornwall deteriorated while a Halifax was far out over the Atlantic, in which case it would be diverted to Lagens, in the Azores, where American engineers had built a large modern runway from which 206 Squadron, re-equipped with B-17 Fortress aircraft, were

'MET' FLIGHTS AND UNUSUAL CARGOES

operating under Coastal Command against U-boats. The Azores Chief Engineer was Col. Dave Morris, of the US Army Air Corps, an old friend from Icelandic days, and 206 Squadron was commanded by W/Cdr 'Butch' Patrick, an old Canadian friend from pre-war days at Bircham. So it was that there existed an Anglo-American friendly triangle, with Cornwall, Gibraltar and the Azores linked by Halifax flights to gain the weather observations on which the operation of Bomber Command against Germany largely depended.

In these circumstances, it would have been less than human if occasional bottles of Spanish sherry had not made the trip from Gibraltar to Norfolk: perhaps after fifty years a story or two may now be told.

During 1943/44 I built up an unofficial, strictly non-profitmaking organisation, through which cases of sherry, usually La Ina, Dry Sack and Tio Pepe, were airlifted to VIPs such as Air Chief Marshal Sir Richard Peirse in India, Air Marshal Sir Geoffrey Bromet in the Azores, and so on. This was really just an extension of what the Royal Navy had been doing for generations. It involved no extra flights and brought a certain style and dignity to the life of senior RAF officers operating in remote places where normal supplies of such commodities were non-existent. It also brought some agonising moments, for example when one engine of a Catalina failed and the flying boat had to be lightened by jettisoning all non-essential equipment, like two cases of La Ina sherry!

On another occasion, two cases of sherry were stored overnight in the orderly room at RAF North Front before being loaded on to an aircraft bound for Lagens. A fortnight later, Sir Geoffrey, on a routine visit to Gibraltar, reported a deficiency of two bottles. Worse than this even, their place in the case had been taken by two rolled-up green folders of information labelled 'Confidential', obviously grabbed from the nearest office tray, wrapped in the paper from the bottles and stuffed into the empty places. No one had reported any files missing and, on a technicality, this could have had serious consequences. In fact, their contents were of no consequence and, in any case, they were safely back in the cabinet without really having been compromised. I did tighten up on security after that; of sherry and of files. In truth, ninety-five per cent of papers labelled 'Secret' or 'Confidential' at that time could have been published in the local paper without damage.

My friendly organisation involved inter-service cooperation, and on one occasion while in the Azores for a few days, I located a large stock of Coates' Plymouth Gin (pre-Blitz) in the naval base store. As it happened, I had often heard Vice-Admiral Sir Harold Burrough (Flag Officer Gibraltar and Mediterranean Approaches) complain that the main stocks of real Plymouth gin had been destroyed during the German air raids on Plymouth in 1941, and that the new stocks were much inferior. I bought and paid for two cases on the spot and arranged for them to be delivered to 'The Mount' in Gibraltar via the next armed trawler to be sent to the dockyard for a boiler clean. Such matters (the gin purchase, not the boiler clean) were handled discreetly between 'Flags' and me, and in due course the Flag Lieutenant gave me a cheque, with no open comment by either party. Incidents such as this greatly helped RN/RAF cooperation, and hence, the war effort.

We sometimes hear about 'rackets' and of course there is potential for evil as well as good when official boundaries are stepped over. Here is a story of a very modest racket which did no harm to anyone.

206 Squadron, in the Azores, had to send their Fortress aircraft to the UK for major inspections and engine changes, and necessarily the aircrews had to take a week's leave at

home in the process. No pineapples were officially imported into the UK in war time, but some wealthy people longed to have a pineapple gracing their fruit bowl at Claridge's or some West End dinner party. Thus the price of pineapples at Covent Garden rose to over five pounds. Yet in the Azores a really magnificent pineapple cost the equivalent of sixpence to one shilling (less than five pence today), so a kitbag full enabled a humble Sgt Air Gunner to have a really good weekend in Town. In 1944/45, five pounds was quite a lot of money. The Air Marshals had their sherry and the NCOs had their pineapples! Why not?

There were amusing incidents as well. On one trip to the Azores I had my own helmet with integral intercom and oxygen mask to plug in when weather observations were being taken at 19,000 feet. Our wartime aircraft did not have the pressurized hulls that make modern flying so comfortable. Although travelling on duty, I was technically a passenger, and when the intercom of the wireless operator went US, I was morally bound to exchange headsets with him, as he needed the mike and headphones and I only the oxygen. Alas, that W/Op. was a garlic-chewer and I had to choose between oxygen plus garlic or no oxygen. I chose the latter, and at 15,000 feet and above lay flat out on the deck, almost passing out at 18,000 feet; but, with loosened collar and complete inactivity, the moment passed and within an hour we were down to a reasonable altitude and once again I could sit up and then walk around.

Mention of garlic reminds me of another harmless little racket. During the war the importation of garlic cloves went the way of pineapples, and the price of garlic bulbs in Soho restaurants soared sky-high. A little garlic goes a long way, and a haversack full of garlic bought in Spain or Gibraltar for almost nothing would pay for two days' leave in London – it was just a question of finding the right contact in Soho.

Banana imports, needing specialised ships not available during the war, ceased abruptly in 1939. By 1945 it was said that young people had forgotten what they were like, and could not even understand the point of old jokes about 'slipping on a banana skin'. In those days children suffering from coeliac disease were said to make a swifter recovery on a diet including bananas, so we made a point of loading them whenever possible. Actually they reacted badly to low temperatures (as in an aircraft at high altitude) and were not always in good condition when they arrived. Anyway, we did our best and sent them automatically to the nearest hospital in the UK and received letters of thanks.

26

Save us from our friends – II

The sun was setting behing Algeciras as our Leigh Light Wellington (179 Squadron) took off from Gibraltar's North Front airstrip and banked gently to port, past the dockyard, past the Old Naval Hospital (now housing Wrens), past Europa Point and into the open Med. Away from the Rock and the hills behind Algeciras, the sun was now higher than we had realised and we had at least an hour of good light before reaching our patrol area. Our mission was to pick up by radar a possible U-boat at night and home in quickly at low level, lowering our huge searchlight in its housing below the fuselage and switching on when just over a mile away on an attacking run with depth-charges. Usually the contact turned out to be a Spanish tunny-fishing boat – how surprised they must have been when suddenly caught in a searchlight appearing out of the sky. At this moment we could see two or three such boats fishing about 3,000 feet below. The coast of Spain was clearly visible to port and accurately ranged by our 10 cm. radar, so navigation was easy. Hitler was trying to get more U-boats into the Mediterranean, we understood, and one of them had been D/F'd by W/T* last night, southeast of Malaga, so for another hour we could relax. That afternoon on Sandy Bay had been sheer bliss. The warm water, hot sun and scorching white sand: and Wrens off watch from Cipher Room soaking up the sun before the next spell on duty under 1,200 feet of solid limestone.

Dee and Mhairie were going to the library dance that night and we had said that we might see them before the end if we were back in time, but this did not seem very likely now and probably two of the 25,000 gallant men in khaki would be taking care of them instead.

Night anti-U-boat patrols had not been much use before, but the new searchlight technique had changed all that and the radar altimeter gave one the confidence to come down to seventy-five feet, or even fifty, on the darkest night before switching the Leigh Light on a radar contact a mile ahead.

'What's that vessel dead ahead, John? She looks a bit long for a coaster.'

'I dunno, it's getting darkish and she ought to be wearing her lights now. Look. she's signalling – *dot, dot, dot, dot, dot.* What's the "letter of the day"? Is it "H"?'

'No, it's "A", flash them on the Aldis, it looks like one of our destroyers.'

'Hell, it's tracer, they're not signalling, they're shooting!'

As the Wellington banked steeply to port the orange sparks floated lazily up and then seemed to defy the natural laws of gravity and came faster and faster until they flashed past a

---

*'D/F'd by W/T' refers to location by intercepted radio signal. U-boats surfaced at night to recharge batteries and communicate with their headquarters. The Admiralty operated a chain of monitoring stations taking bearings on these transmissions. The intersection of such bearings gave a position (within a few miles).

hundred yards away and curved over slowly behind us. Then a dull red flash from the destroyer, and another.

'Put her nose down, for Christ's sake, or we've had it.'

'*Crump, crump*' and at the same time, a most horrible jangling rattle, and the whole aircraft shook as a four-inch shell exploded under the port wing. We dived to sea-level and to the west, to get away from all this.

'It was our fault, you know, Prof, we came out of the setting sun on an attacking course directly over that ship.'

'Yes, but Ops. said nothing about any friendly destroyer and this one certainly was not on the plot. Anyway, we can argue about this afterwards, let's get back first.'

The port fuel tanks were holed but starboard gauges were showing OK. It was about 150 miles to Gibraltar and we were not all that worried. Then the port engine started dropping revs, so we gained all the height we could and broke W/T silence with a position signal.

'Starboard inner tank has also gone, skipper, we shall be lucky to make it.'

'OK – warn North Front for a crash landing.'

The Wellington flew gamely on and even gained a few hundred feet so that depth-charges could be safely jettisoned. The one good engine gave a lovely, even note. La Linea was a blaze of light by now and the cheerful voice of North Front Flying Control was reassuring. We rumbled in over the sea and put down on the runway, swinging violently round as a damaged tyre stripped off. Fortunately the runway is exceptionally wide and there was nothing in the way. A Hillman 15-cwt. truck picked us up and in Ops. we were very brief.

'We can always look at the aircraft in the morning but right now it's 9 o'clock and we're due at a dance, chaps.'

Next day, Naval Ops. gave me two pink signal slips which I still cherish – 'FOGMA from SLAZAK. Am being attacked by one Ju 88 in position so-and-so. T.O.O. 19.22,' and 'FOGMA from SLAZAK. Report one enemy aircraft shot down in sea. Am investigating T.O.O. 19.25.'

The *Slazak* was a 'friendly' Polish destroyer working with us, but not based on Gibraltar. They were not familiar with Wellingtons flying around and we understood their reaction, hoping one day to have a drink with them perhaps, but alas our paths never crossed again.

27

The Condors of KG40

Mention has been made already of a Russian convoy shadowed by a long-range Focke Wulf 200 (Condor) aircraft; this would have been based at Trondheim in Norway, but the main base of KG 40 (the squadron or wing operating these four-engined aircraft) was at Bordeaux/Merignac, in France.

The Germans were slow to develop new aircraft and obviously hoped to win the war with the Heinkel 111, Dornier Do 17 and Junkers Ju 88 (twin-engined bomber), together with the Junkers Ju 87 dive bomber and the Messerschmitt Me 109 fighter (single-engined) as well as the Me 110 long-range fighter. But the war went on longer than they expected, and while we had several long-range aircraft, like the four-engined Sunderland and Catalina flying boats, as well as land planes, in 1943/44 the enemy had only the FW 200 Condor, adapted from civil airlines, plus some He 111s fitted with extra fuel tanks. For such reasons, the Condors were used mainly for long-range reconnaissance, spotting and shadowing our convoys well out in the Atlantic and passing the information on to U-boats. They were also sometimes used for attacks on convoys but very sensibly operated only where our fighter aircraft were not expected. For most of the war (after the fall of France), the main force was at Bordeaux, with a detached flight at Trondheim. In fact, they operated round trips from Bordeaux to Trondheim and vice versa, well out into the Atlantic. While stationed in Iceland, I became aware of this squadron when on rare occasions they flew in our area; their main interest was in shipping, especially the fortnightly convoys to Russia.

In our RAF Intelligence office, deep inside the Rock of Gibraltar, we kept a careful plot of all FW 200 sightings reported by our shipping over several months, and the pattern of activity became very clear, with a well-defined arc of sightings at the limit of their range. Once a convoy hundreds of miles out into the Atlantic had reported a sighting, we came to expect either a pack of U-boats to gather on the route ahead, or possibly a high-level bombing attack by up to six Condors within two or three days.

Quite by chance one evening, I met a quietly spoken Flight Lieutenant signals officer over a drink at the Rock Hotel. He seemed to be stationed on top of the Rock, in charge of a W/T station. I checked up on him with our chief signals officer and was told, 'Oh, he's nothing to do with us. He works for the Air Ministry – listening to German radio or something like that.' I was intrigued and cultivated his acquaintance. What he told me was most interesting. He was in charge of a 'Y Unit', a radio intelligence set-up reporting direct to the Air Ministry in London, i.e. long-term strategic intelligence. From him I learned that his wireless operators had developed a personal interest in transmissions from Bordeaux/Merignac concerning the operation of Kg 40 and their Condors. He told me that they could even recognise the 'personal signatures' of the individual German 'colleagues' from the rhythm and nature of their Morse keying.

Apparently it was the German custom that these aircraft should exchange call-signs with base shortly after take-off, to confirm that their radio was working efficiently. I realised immediately that here was a gold-mine of tactical intelligence apparently not envisaged by the Air Ministry in London, and had a 'tied line' field telephone put in from my office to the office of my friend at the top of the Rock. At first I had occasional calls which we tried to link with FW 200 sightings, and then I would ask (as a favour!) for a special watch at certain times. Within a short time it was possible to correlate an intercepted 'W/T Go!' with actual flights, and when a report of six such intercepts within ten minutes was received, I had a hunch that they would be attacking a certain convoy, already known to have been sighted by an FW 200 the previous day. I at once called in at the Met. Office down the corridor, for a 'Met. wind' (wind speed and direction between Bordeaux and the possible target) and applied this to the known cruising speed of the Condors. It seemed that they would be at the convoy at about 1210 hours. I then walked into the big naval Ops. Room, explained the situation to the duty Commander and suggested that he make a signal to the Senior Naval Officer of the convoy escort: 'Expect attack by six FW 200 aircraft e.t.a. 12 noon'. The first response was, 'I can't do that! How can you possibly be so sure?' I think he spoke to someone in the Admiral's office, who suggested that he did what Brown said.

I also pointed out that the naval escort included two AA cruisers, *Scylla* and *Charybdis*, and that the convoy would have almost three hours' notice so that ships could be disposed for defence against air attack rather than U-boat attack. In other words, spread out more widely, perhaps with an AA cruiser at each end instead of being more bunched, to enable anti-submarine escorts to protect them to best advantage. I had more tact than to suggest such a response, naturally! For the rest of the morning, I was so excited that I could think of nothing else. Then at 1205 hours came a signal from SNO: 'Am being attacked by five aircraft.' This was followed by a later signal:

'Enemy aircraft driven off by gunfire. No damage to convoy.'

My friend on top of the Rock later confirmed that one Condor arrived back at Bordeaux two hours before the others, perhaps with engine trouble. Two days later the destroyer escort put into Gibraltar, having been relieved by others for the next part of the trip into the Mediterranean. Three naval officers reported to their Ops. Room and were told, 'Go and talk to the RAF about it.' I was delighted to meet three very satisfied customers, very curious to know more and obviously thinking that we had a spy in Bordeaux! I just had to say, 'Please, don't ask any more. You wouldn't want a brave man to lose his life over this, would you?'

At this stage in the war there were also some small but important convoys sailing from Lisbon round to Gibraltar. I believe they carried such cargoes as watch mechanisms and optical devices of various kinds, for plotting contours from stereo pairs of vertical air photos, as well as binoculars and so on, which I would have thought could have been flown in anyway. I suspect there were other items not known to us, coming from Switzerland. These convoys were not difficult for German long-range aircraft to find off the Portuguese coast, especially as Lisbon, a neutral city, had many German agents. After one occasion when serious losses were sustained,

I suggested to the AOC that if we could have a detached flight of Beaufighters at Gib for a few weeks, with our intelligence technique we could deploy these long-range fighters over the next convoy.

There was no question of continuous fighter patrols at such long range, but with accurate timing I calculated that a Beaufighter could stay fifteen-twenty minutes with the convoy and still have a combat endurance margin plus fuel for return to Gibraltar. Those small convoys must have been more valuable than I believed, for HQ Coastal Command agreed and sent us a detached flight of four Beaufighters.

Luck was with us, and within a few days the next convoy was attacked off Cape Sines, about sixty miles south of Lisbon, and a flight of our three fighters arrived at the convoy at the same time as four Condors! One was shot down in flames into the sea in full view of our ships (a good morale-booster!) one crashed in Portugal (I obtained photographs from local sources), and the other two were both damaged but struggled back to Bordeaux. After this, there were no more air attacks on the Lisbon convoys – the large four-engined FW 200s were far too valuable for long-range reconnaissances to be risked within reach of enemy fighters.

Sadly, one Beaufighter failed to return.

28
Flying airships with the US Navy

Mankind first flew some 200 years ago, in France, using both hot-air and hydrogen-filled balloons; the latter were used in war as long ago as 1870, by the French in the siege of Paris. In the First World War, London was bombed by German airships (Zeppelins) and we ourselves made extensive use of hydrogen balloons for artillery observation in static trench warfare. On a very limited scale we also used a few small airships for naval reconnaissance. During the 1920s and 1930s, a number of giant airships were built and operated, but sadly were abandoned after a series of disastrous fires and explosions.

During the last ten years a few small airships have been produced, all filled with helium, a gas not quite as light as hydrogen but completely non-inflammable.

So far as I know, the only airships used in the Second World War were the US Naval Blimps, based on Port Lyautey, in French Morocco, on the Atlantic coast, and well away from any enemy aircraft. Basically, these had an outer envelope of 3-ply rubberised fabric holding 450,000 cub. ft. of helium with separate ballonets of air for pressure regulation. Powered by two Pratt and Whitney Wasp 450-hp. engines giving a cruising speed of fifty five-sixty knots and a maximum speed of seventy five-eighty knots, they had a very long endurance, but usually flew for about fifteen hours on each sortie.

Up to about twenty years ago, helium was a very rare and expensive gas, and in 1944 we had to be very careful not to lose any by flying too high. The design provided for this by having separate ballonets made in the form of huge cylinders or drums with flexible ends. At ground level helium only filled about eighty per cent of the available volume, so that the ballonet ends were concave, to allow for considerable expansion without loss of gas.

At 6,000 feet, air pressure is only four-fifths, or eighty per cent, of that at ground level (your household barometer would indicate twenty-four inches instead of thirty). At this pressure the helium would expand to fill a space proportionately larger and the ballonet ends would be convex, gently pressing against each other, completely filling all available space. Any further expansion, caused by flying higher than 6,000 feet (our so-called 'pressure height'), would result in loss of helium, and had to be avoided.

When fully loaded with gasoline and bombs, each blimp had a negative buoyancy of 600–800 lb. But after a fifteen-hour flight had a positive buoyancy of over 800 lb. (much more, of course, if bombs had been dropped). For protection against wind and weather, they were normally housed in hangars, but could also be moored from tall masts in the open; in fact we had a mooring-mast for a blimp erected at Europa Point, Gibraltar, but it was seldom used.

For take-off, a blimp was hauled out by a ground crew, its apparent 600-lb. weight taken by a wheel in the bows. Take-off was very similar to that of a normal aircraft, into wind up the runway, with nose down and engines revved up. When an airspeed of about thirty knots was reached, the tail was brought down by elevator control and the ship took off. Coming home fifteen hours later with positive buoyancy, one had to approach up-wind and fly them down; without power, they tended to go up, not down like aeroplanes. So, when the nosewheel touched down on the runway, a ground crew of eight men was waiting to catch the two lines ejected (one each side) and hold the ship down until sandbags were placed on external hooks as ballast. In flight, one can always make the ship lighter by throwing something overboard (somebody, if really necessary!), but it is very difficult to gain weight, except perhaps in a heavy shower of rain, when the weight of water on the huge suface area can build up quickly.

The crew and equipment were housed in a spacious gondola under the envelope, with the two engines well away, high on either side of the main structure. It took two men to fly it: the 'helmsman' sat in front with a rigid control column, much like that of a car, controlling the rudder only; the 'elevator man' sat immediately behind him, with a large wheel on his right, plus a foot clutch. This wheel had a rubber rim and reminded me of the wheel of an invalid chair; it was in much the same position.

To bring the nose up to gain height, one had to declutch and wind the wheel back from the top. This raised the elevator surfaces on the tailplane so that the slipstream pushed the tail down. Conversely, one wound the wheel forwards to bring the nose down and lose height. The direction of flight was controlled by the rudder, actuated by the 'helmsman' via the central column.

When I first took over on a flight as 'elevator man', we were flying at about a hundred feet and I was told to bring her up and hold her steady at our normal operational height of 150 feet above sea level. I wound the wheel back and waited two or three seconds, then wound back some more, but nothing seemed to happen, so I wound back still more. Then the nose slowly came up and I moved the wheel forward to level out, but still the nose came up! One had no response or 'feel' of the controls, as with an aircraft, and it needed experience to 'steer small' and make small corrections. I have never steered a 200,000-ton oil tanker, but I can well imagine the same lack of response there, as opposed to steering a fourteen-foot dinghy. The difference was much more than that of handling a four-engined Stirling bomber after flying a Tiger Moth. Fortunately, airships are more 'forgiving' than aeroplanes, and I soon learned the new technique.

The gondola of an airship was very comfortable, with plenty of room to walk about and reclining chairs in which to relax or sleep when off watch. Cooking facilities were excellent. For example, on one night flight, I remember a wonderful dinner, about an hour after take-off: chicken à la Maryland (with sweetcorn), followed by apple pie with cream and ice-cream and then a mug of excellent Costa Rican coffee. Throughout the long night there was a cup of coffee or hot soup every two hours and around 0730 hours I was asked if I wanted my eggs 'over and under' or 'sunny side up' – with ham, perhaps?

To get back to serious matters, these US Naval Blimps had been fitted with the same Magnetic Airborne Detector (MAD) systems as had one Catalina flying-boat squadron based at Gibraltar (known as the 'MAD CATS'). These were large and sensitive magnetometer loops, fitted in the hull (the wings, in the case of Catalinas), which could detect anomalies in the earth's magnetic field, e.g. flux changes induced by large iron or steel objects up to many hundreds of feet away. When flying at 150 feet above sea level this meant that a steel U-boat hull as much as 600 feet below the water surface would produce a 'kick' or sudden deflection on the magnetometer dial as we flew over it, unseen and unseeing.

Obviously, any object, bomb or marker buoy, released as the magnetometer recorded a 'contact' would overshoot, as it would travel forward in a parabola with the same speed as the airship for about three or four seconds before entering the water. So our buoys (and bombs) were fitted with retro rockets, or short tubes of slow-burning cordite in the nose, to push them backwards and exactly neutralise the forward speed, thus making them fall vertically downwards to the spot where they should go. This had the added advantage of allowing the aircraft to be further away before the bombs exploded. The bombs were fitted with hydrostatic fuses, activated by water pressure to explode at any desired depth, pre-set; this gave yet a few seconds more for us to get away from the huge upburst of water when the 'depth-bombs' exploded, as well as being more efficient against submerged targets.

We had a crew of two officers and six senior NCOs. At any given time there would be two flying the ship, one watching the radar screen and the magnetometer, and a radio operator. We flew on pre-determined tracks to cover the Western Approaches and, with clear radar echoes from both Spanish and African coastlines, navigation was very straightforward. Usually, two crew at a time were relaxing off-duty for about three hours.

Although this particular trip was uneventful, I have a very clear memory of the attacking procedure. Should the magnetometer indicate a 'contact', a fluorescent marker fitted with retro-burner was dropped immediately, staining the sea a bright yellow over an area which soon spread to almost two hundred yards across. The airship at once turned to port and flew in a complete circle of a radius of about two miles, with the yellow patch at the centre. Six retro radio buoys were dropped at equal intervals on this turn; each buoy had a listening hydrophone in the water and a radio aerial above, transmitting at slightly different frequencies. We had a facility for press-button tuning to listen to them all in quick succession, in the hope and expectation of a hydrophone effect (HE) from some of them, and hoping to distinguish one HE much stronger than the rest. If two were equally strong and the others very much less, then the U-boat's track would roughly be bisecting the angle between the two, out from the yellow patch, thus giving a clue to the apparent track of the target. The airship would then make an attacking run on this track, ready to drop a stick of four 350-lb. depth-bombs, set to explode at fifty, seventy-five, 150 and 250 feet, on a strong magnetometer contact. On a weaker contact, two further radio buoys would be dropped instead, to give a better indication of the track, and another attacking run made. Even more up-to-date was the sonar buoy, with a miniaturised sonar ('Asdic' to the Royal Navy) to pick up echoes from an object rather than propeller noises. During all this procedure, the U-boat, perhaps making five knots at sixty feet below, would be quite unaware of our presence.

If a U-boat were detected on the surface, the role of an airship was not to attack but to cruise around just out of range, transmitting details of position to base, and wait for two B–24 (Liberators to us) aircraft to fly out from Port Lyautey at high speed to attack simultaneously from opposite directions, with their much superior fire power from four twenty-mm. cannon firing forward, plus A/S bombs, of course. Normally one or two destroyers would also come out, if not too far away, to carry on the hunt with their sonar equipment, should the U-boat crash-dive. At this time (1944) U-boats were getting better defensive fire power, with a quadruple twenty-mm. turret or, alternatively, one or a pair of thirty-seven-mm. AA guns.

Technical data:
(i) *Hydrophone Effect* (HE) is the noise of rotating propellers transmitted through the sea and picked up by a microphone under water.
(ii) *Helium*, almost as light as hydrogen, was formerly obtained only from natural gas found almost entirely in the USA. It was then rare and expensive, much more costly than hydrogen. Nowadays it is obtained very cheaply as a by-product of oxygen by the fractional distillation of liquid air. Normal air contains five parts per million of helium.
(iii) *Magnetometer* loops are wide coils of thin insulated wire, which generate a small electric current when moved through a magnetic field, even that of the earth's magnetism. A large iron or steel object (like a submarine) will concentrate the earth's magnetic field and produce a bigger current, indicated on a sensitive instrument.

29
Battle of the Strait of Gibraltar

It was appreciated that the enemy would attempt to reinforce his Mediterranean U-boat fleet, which since the collapse of Italy had been well below the strength necessary to threaten

Allied shipping at all seriously. Such attempts had so far been only partially successful, scarcely making good normal operational wastage: for example, between 24 October and 2 November 1943 five U-boats attempted the passage; three were sunk by surface and air attack, only two reaching Toulon.

At the end of December 1943 there were signs that U-boats were again trying to force the Strait, but intensive air and surface A/S patrols to prevent this failed to produce any satisfactory results. It did become clear from eight daylight sightings by transit aircraft, as well as from four night attacks by Leigh Light Wellingtons of 179 Squadron and one by a destroyer (all between 7 and 10 January 1944) that some U-boats had got through. All these sightings were about thirty miles off the Spanish coast, between Cape de Gata and Cape Não (150–300 miles east of Gibraltar). These were consistent with newly arrived U-boats making their way to their base at Toulon.

Our aircraft making night attacks reported a much more efficient and determined AA defence by these U-boats, now equipped with quadruple 20-mm. guns, and possibly with specially picked or unusually well-trained crews, for this second attempt. One U-boat in particular shot down Wellington R/179 and damaged two others, yet survived all three attacks: F/O Davidson (Captain and sole survivor of the downed Wellington) reported that twenty minutes later the U-boat almost collided with his rubber dinghy. At this time, 2300 hours, he had presumably not been seen. However, the Germans asked the Spanish on 9 January to search for survivors from a U-boat said to have sunk off Aguilas (northeast of Cape de Gata) on the night of the 8th/9th and, although a search by two Spanish ships produced no results, the inference is that one U-boat was sunk.

mise condensation drops of cold water down necks!). For me, it was absolutely fascinating to be on the receiving end of depth-charges, to hear that dramatic, echoing clang as of metal on metal and to see the lights flicker.

We had planned to cruise submerged at different depths, at a constant two knots to give reasonable trimming control, so that our attendant vessel could monitor our actual speed 'over the ground' at various states of the tide. In the event, we found a boundary layer, or density layer, about 200 feet down, with a sudden change of water temperature; at this boundary layer there was so much turbulence that the seaman trimming the boat was unable to keep her level on hydroplanes and we found ourselves unwillingly at 350 feet and still angled downwards, with ominous creakings (and more cork dust!). I had assumed all this to be normal, but when I saw an experienced Chief Petty Officer looking worried, I felt worried, too. He said that in fifteen years with submarines he had never been below 300 feet before. I said, 'But U-boats go down to 600 feet,' and he replied, 'Ours aren't built to do that.' However, by increasing revs to give us four–six knots we regained control. It was interesting to learn afterwards that this turbulent boundary layer made Asdic detection more difficult, if not impossible. To me, an unexpected feature after several hours was my personal loss of concentration, similar to that experienced in an aircraft at 16,000 feet and above without an oxygen mask. I was told that there was no acute oxygen shortage, but in discussion with RAF medical officers afterwards it was explained to me that in an atmosphere of 100 per cent relative humidity, as in the confined space of a submarine, human lungs failed to effect oxygen/carbon dioxide exchange efficiently, probably on account of a film of moisture on the lungs' alveolar cells. My mind went back to U–570, which had a most efficient de-humidifier. This bal-

Obviously, these enemy tactics produced much thought on how best to plan our air sorties, but we did not have enough knowledge of currents in the Strait and how these might affect the passage of submarines. Negative results from night patrols by Leigh Light Wellingtons produced evidence that, as might be expected, the U-boats were getting through submerged. We had to estimate the likely points west, where they were submerging, and east, where they would be surfacing. We had full information on endurance and cruising speeds of U-boats, both submerged and on the surface. Indeed, we had captured U 570 off Iceland in August 1941 (*see* Chapter 13) and only recently I had enjoyed a long chat with Lt. Cdr Marriott, who had commanded U–570 (re-named HMS *Graph*) in action against her former owners. Now, by chance, he was commanding HMS *Stoic* on passage to the Far East and was staying a few days at Gib for stores.

In my office next to the Main Operations Room, off the Admiralty tunnel in the middle of the Rock, I kept a large wall-map of the Russia front, amended daily. On most mornings, Admiral Burrough and his Flag Lieutenant looked in to discuss this, as we had both seen action on Russian convoys. I suggested to Sir Harold that it would help enormously if we could get a friendly submarine to play the part of a U-boat trying to enter the Med. and find out how he would plan to do it. He agreed at once and invited me to make the trip. Thus it was that I found myself in HMS *Stoic* for twelve hours travelling submerged through the narrows from just east of Cape Spartel to just east of Gibraltar. We had a small attendant escort vessel keeping Asdic contact, but for an hour or so in the middle she lost contact and dropped small depth-charges to let us know where she was. One of these was too close for comfort and produced a shower of cork particles down our necks (hull interiors were lined with cork to mini-

anced the atmosphere in the boat and also produced several gallons of distilled water as a useful by-product. My respect for the enemy increased still further.

Some of the known factors operating on the waters of the Strait should perhaps be listed:

(a) The Med. is virtually tideless east of Alboran Island, about 100 miles east of Gibraltar. At Gibraltar the tide is about three feet, off Tarifa about four-and-a-half feet and twice as much west of Cape Spartel.
(b) The water in the Med. is usually several degrees (12–16° Fahrenheit) warmer than the Atlantic water west of the Strait. A strong west wind seems to bring colder water around to Gibraltar after a couple of days (personal observation, from daily swims off Sandy Bay on east side of the Rock).
(c) The Med. loses by evaporation about three times as much water as it receives through rain and run-off via rivers. Thus there is a net overall inflow of water from the Atlantic.
(d) Since water in the Med. is more saline, and so denser, there is an outward flow at depths ranging from 200 feet downwards.
(e) At the narrowest point the Strait of Gibraltar is only just over eight nautical miles wide, i. e. just under ten land miles. Even between Ceuta (on the north African coast) and Gibraltar, the two 'Pillars of Hercules', the distance is only fourteen land miles. The depth of water varies greatly, but is mostly 2,000 feet even close inshore, and much more in places.

The implications for diesel/electric U-boats trying to get through the Strait submerged by night became much clearer after theoretical appraisal was reinforced by practical experiments in HMS *Stoic*. This helped in the tactical planning of our blockade.

The boundary layer referred to was, of course, no obstacle to U-boat detection by our Catalina flying boats and US Naval Blimps fitted with MAD gear (see p. 122) and by the end of 1944 we felt that at last we were able to keep U-boat reinforcements from entering the Med.

30

General Montgomery seen in Gibraltar

Military intelligence has been defined as 'the collection, collation and dissemination of information about the enemy'. It also involves another aspect, the occasional and timely planting of disinformation about ourselves and in Gibraltar, we were singularly well placed for this second role.

In the run-up to the Normandy landings it was perceived that, if the enemy became aware that General Montgomery was secretly visiting north Africa, they might suppose that the 'Second Front' was unlikely to begin without him in the immediate future. So, as we know, impersonated by actor Clifton James, he was 'seen' as passing via Gibraltar on his way to Algiers. My small part in this was to arrange for Commandante Molina (Spanish Air Force) to be visiting Gibraltar as our guest at this time. I also arranged for Gerry, my most fluent Spanish-speaking officer to be showing him around RAF North Front at the time when the VIP York was expected to arrive from the UK. As the York touched down and a staff car drove alongside on the runway to collect a passenger discreetly, Gerry tried to divert Molina's attention to a Mosquito aircraft (at that time the fastest bomber in the RAF) but Molina had caught a glimpse of a familiar figure in a beret and suddenly remembered an important engagement in Spain. The false 'Monty' had a meal at the 'Convent' (Government House) with the Governor and proceeded next morning to Maison Blanche airfield, Algiers, where he disappeared into the desert, having been noted there, I believe. A week later he came back in civilian clothes in a very plain Dakota and had a meal with me before returning to the UK.

We were delighted when our radio 'Y service' at the top of the Rock intercepted a special transmission from the German observation post in La Linea, reporting the secret passage of the great General Montgomery through Gibraltar. The Second Front in Europe started a day or two later, with a considerable element of tactical surprise.

There had been other and more ambitious deception techniques – for example, the body 'washed ashore' in Spain not far from Gibraltar, with papers falsely indicating our invasion plans. This was publicised in the press (THE MAN WHO NEVER WAS) just after the war and has been frequently written about, but so far as I know the details mentioned here have not been published before.

As general background, I should mention that Commandante Molina was known by us to be very pro-German and occasionally involved in the regular bulletins of military activity (sea, air, land) observed on the Rock. These were normally made by a twenty-four hour observation station in

La Linea, equipped with a powerful binocular telescope. All aircraft taking off and landing at North Front runway, all flying boats and shipping movements in and out of the harbour, were methodically noted. The Germans (or their Spanish employees) broadcast a very thorough bulletin to Germany every eight hours; this gave all our movements with the most admirable accuracy. As we had no such complete list ourselves, I had transcripts made of these 'Y'-sevice intercepts and copied to Governor and C.-in-C., FOGMA (the Admiral) and AOC. These gentlemen often said that they picked up movements of our own forces which had passed by unnoticed by them and were quick to phone me if the regular bulletin was not on their desk. In passing, perhaps I should mention 'Operation Chickfeed'. This was a collection of small intelligence items about our own forces which we didn't particularly worry about or knew that they would find out soon anyway. Such tit bits were fed innocently to DAs (double agents) and known pro-Germans in Spain in order to maintain their credibility, so that an occasional 'clanger' of disinformation could be dropped in from time to time.

One serious difficulty arose over a court-martial. The mail of service personnel was censored and of course any information about our own ship movements was officially secret and not to be mentioned. A soldier gave the name of a British fourteen-inch battleship arriving at Gibraltar and was put on a court-martial charge! We knew that the enemy were as aware of all such things as we were, in the peculiar situation of the Rock, and I felt that I had to have a quiet word with the Judge Advocate-General's department, to let the victim down as lightly as possible. Definitely not a case for a firing squad!

31

Per Minimis Ad Astra

One of the less likeable characteristics of the RAF was the dogged way in which some administrative officers would follow through with procedural details, regardless of bigger issues, in peace and in war. I suppose it could be argued that this prevented corruption and helped to keep us all on the straight-and-narrow. Here are four examples.

Before the war, as Station Education Officer, I held the inventory of the library and (though no longer in Education) still had it in 1940/41 when F/O Bulloch (later awarded the DSO and Bar) wanted to borrow a seldom-used book, *Norries' Nautical Tables*. This was to help him with his navigation (he was a ferry pilot of new aircraft supplied by the USA at the time, and nothing could have been more important to the war effort). I found and lent him the book at once, but apparently failed to get his signature on a loan card. While serving in Iceland in 1941/42 I received two letters about this, and then a W/T signal to our Chief Signals Officer came in, instructing him to ask me 'If I could throw any light on the disappearance of this book'. Once again I replied that it had been borrowed by someone who made very good use of it, and asked them to contact Sqn Ldr. Bulloch direct (he was already well known for his success against U-boats). I then forgot all about it; but months later a Form 664B was raised against me and followed me to north Russia in 1943. I lost it, but another reached me in Gibraltar in 1944 and I finally signed the bloody thing and the cost was docked from my pay! For non-service readers, this form was in use (possibly still is) to recover the cost of any service equipment lost by a member of the RAF. An enemy bomb on the Education Block at Bircham Newton early in the war could have saved me, but alas the building was never even damaged and nothing could be written off. It was OK to lose an aircraft worth many thousands of pounds, but a book – oh no!

Then there was the occasion at Bircham Newton, at the height of the Battle of Britain, when a Flight Sergeant of 206 Squadron was court-martialled for stealing petrol, after investigators had 'dipped' his car petrol tank and the sample was found to contain high-octane aviation fuel. It was assumed that he had been 'milking a Bowser', i. e. improperly draining petrol from an aircraft refuelling tanker. He was a conscientious man and explained to me that he had used his own car to drive to the satellite airfield to work on a Hudson aircraft grounded there, when no service transport had been available. His Flight Commander backed him up, saying that he was a first-class NCO working flat out to keep aircraft serviceable, and asked me to defend him. I had a certain reputation as a 'bush lawyer' in those days and readily agreed; I enjoyed tackling professional advocates in open court. They had the advantage in legal knowledge and training, but I knew more about the RAF.

On the fateful day I called two expert witnesses: first, the Station Accounts Officer to explain the official system whereby RAF officers and senior NCOs could buy petrol from the Motor Transport Section, on prepayment to RAF Accounts to obtain a voucher. Second, the Station Engineer Officer, to ask whether any aircraft had been damaged during the two weeks prior to the alleged offence, and if so what had been done with any fuel salvaged from their tanks. The answers were, 'Two aircraft in the last twelve days,' and, 'This fuel is not allowed to be supplied to an aircraft for safety reasons. It is pumped into the MT bulk petrol tank.' When asked, 'In your opinion, could such aviation fuel added to the MT tank in this way account for the analysis given here in evidence today?' the answer was, 'Yes, sir, most certainly.' The learned Judge Advocate stopped the case, made some comment about wasting the time of the court, acknowledged the embarrassed apology of King's Counsel prosecuting and gave the defendant an honourable discharge. I suppose, in a way, such fine attention to correct procedure while we were fighting with our backs to the wall in the summer of 1940 was praiseworthy, and in the event justice was done anyway.

Not long after this, I was asked to defend a young Pilot Officer who had damaged his aircraft while landing at St Mawgan, in Cornwall, at dusk. He was charged 'That he did take off from RAF Station Bircham Newton too late to land in daylight at RAF Station St Mawgan, well knowing that he was not night-trained on this type of aircraft'. A young King's Counsel in RAF uniform was the prosecuting officer (from the office of the Judge Advocate-General); he called expert witness as to the distance between RAF Bircham Newton, the cruising speed of the Glenn Martin and the wind speed and direction at the time. In cross-examination I asked for the times of sunset and civil twilight at St Mawgan, but the witness was unable to answer. I was granted permission to call the Station Meteorological Officer to give this evidence, which he then did. The difference in longitude between St Mawgan and Bircham Newton produced another twenty-three minutes of daylight down in west Cornwall, and the case for the prosecution was based on the defendant's arrival to be fifteen minutes too late. Case dismissed. The learned KC appeared to be unaware of the term 'civil twilight' (sun six degrees below horizon), or of the effect of longitude on local solar time. To be honest, the young P/O was very lucky, as the real reason why he arrived after dusk was that he flew off course to circle the home of his girlfriend in Andover on the way!

Between 1938 and 1942 I became almost addicted to RAF law, and appeared at courts martial on a number of occasions, usually during quiet periods of the war. At first I just defended, but then acted as President if no professional Judge Advocate was available; I enjoyed the mental exercise of giving a judicial and impartial 'summing up', and there never seemed to be any conflict between appearances in court and my primary role of Chief Intelligence Officer. However, in Iceland I went to the well once too often and very nearly came to grief. I had verbally agreed to preside at a court martial but failed to note the date, and in the normal course of my real duties had to fly to Greenland at short notice (*see* Chapter 14) and arrived back to find myself in very hot water. I had not been available at the court martial! I apologized profusely and pleaded the exigencies of the service and the importance of what I had had to do, but was very nearly court-martialled myself! It was put to me that RAF discipline took priority over everything, and that nothing could be more important than the course of justice. Fortunately, the AOC was on my side, but I had to eat very humble pie and decided that playing at Chairman of the Bench was not for me any more. I stuck to this principle ever after, even years after the war working in central Africa, and in retirement these last twenty-nine years. My age for many years has protected me from further invitations!